Vietnam

Hidden Riches of a Magical Land

Jochen Voigt

Contents

1 2

7

8 9

1 Luxury cruise in Halong Bay. **2** Luscious tropical fruits on the Mekong. **3** Flower Hmong woman in Can Cau. **4** Freshly baked baguettes. **5** Ducks in Bac Ha. **6** Cycle parking in Hoi An. **7** Bay of tranquility. **8** "Dalat Palace" – orchids for the guests. **9** Candlelight dinner in the Majestic. **10** Your name in Chinese. **11** Architecture and nature: Evason Hideaway. **12** Coolie hats and cool hats.

One of the most memorable activities for your journey to Vietnam is to sail around Halong Bay and its 3,000 islands on a junk. This enigmatic, tranquil landscape of emerald waters, islands, caves, and grottoes inspires dreams. Here, the legend of the dragon that created the bay by flicking its tail – or strewing a handful of pearls – soon transmutes into a personal fairy tale, for the teller can select a suitable ending. The Vietnamese have two versions of the dragon story, one pugnacious and dynamic, the other tranquil and rarefied. Whichever version you prefer, it's the ideal setting in which to luxuriate in the peace and tranquility of the water world as the junk glides through the beautiful landscape. Over one thousand species of fish and 160 types of coral live in the river along which you sail, in a nature reservation declared by UNESCO as a World Heritage Site. To protect the fragile environment, mooring for excursion boats is restricted to specific locations in this natural paradise, where swimming and kayaking are also permitted.

Halong Bay – an enchanted world of water, rocks, and legends.

Chao Mung Quy Khach Den Viet Nam!

Welcome to Vietnam!

No other country has been unfurled before us by war photographers with such intensity as Vietnam, and none has been so misrepresented. For many people, the memory of these images prevents them from overcoming their fears and ushering in a new perspective, banishing the ghosts of the past, and pointing Vietnam's way into a peaceful future.

And there are plenty of reasons to regard Vietnam from a new perspective. In recent years, the country has increased in popularity as a tourist destination and, despite the slow pace of developments, has succeeded in establishing a place for itself in the international community. Yet Vietnam has remained a country which maintains its traditions and preserves its wonderful culture – and which can once again welcome strangers with genial charm. Visitors rapidly feel at home in Vietnam. No other Asian country offers so many options for carefree, safe traveling. However, the country offers such a vast choice of vacation types, from luxury holidays to cultural and adventure trips, that it is wise to consider personal preferences in advance. These travel chronicles, containing a mixture of up-to-date information, descriptions of wonderful experiences, and brief anecdotes, are aimed at assisting travelers by enabling them to develop a feeling of familiarity with the country and its people before they embark on their own story.

The long, narrow strip of land that is Vietnam offers an enormous range of regional types, from jungles and mountains to endless beaches. Its 1,650 kilometers (990 miles) from the Mekong Delta to the extreme north bordering China are crammed with more rich diversity than any other Asian country. The senses are stimulated anew from region to region, as eyes, ears, and nose vie for attention for the new impressions they collect: scents, sounds, images. A wealth of new pictures of flowers, animals, people, and tranquil scenes have finally replaced the grim images from the news broadcasts that flooded into our homes thirty or forty years ago. Not a trace of weariness arises along these extensive roads; even simple facts gleaned while traveling can amaze and delight. The coffee from the mountain uplands is among the best in the world, the coveted cinnamon from the Yen Bai region ends up in the port of Hamburg, and Vietnam is the country that put the pep in pepper. The perfect place to send anyone who can handle the heat, for Vietnam is a loud country, a bustling, vibrant country, a country which, by our terms, should generate aggression in its inhabitants, but this is not the case. Vietnam's brand of chaos has a calming effect without being stupefying. It mobilizes abilities which have been lost in our world, whether they relate to dealing with others or ourselves. Suddenly our senses are positively wired, no longer engaged in hostile, cutthroat competition as at home, and this change soon takes us over, as we hesitantly return a smile – or, as the change advances, even smile first. This has its consequences, of course, for nowhere in Asia is laughter so hearty and honest as in Vietnam.

Such personal experiences help to flesh out our view of the country. But it draws its personal features from its people, who smooth our path in establishing friendly contact. There is a charming background to this behavior. The Vietnamese are a genial and highly inquisitive people who are keen to find out every detail. A question about your personal life is a sure sign that you've been accepted. Serve up a grimly fascinating tale of weeping children and acrimonious divorce and you have the undivided attention of any Vietnamese. A round of rice wine, snake brandy or green tea on the house rounds off the story –and inspires new ones: ghastly tales of snake soup and stewed dog.

Let's get one thing perfectly clear: Vietnam has everything to offer, and for some travelers, this is exactly what they desperately seek. Yet Vietnam also has traditions which Europeans cannot grasp, but to which they frequently apply a superficial understanding. Snake is a delicacy throughout Asia, and is served up in appetizing dishes at high prices. For this reason no more need be said about the rumors that restaurants are the last resting-place for many a cuddly pet. Tâys, Western foreigners, should drop the subject and turn to more interesting matters. For example, the absorbing question of how to describe Vietnam's shape on the map. Europeans tend to compare the outline of the country to a sea horse facing the Gulf of Tonking and nestling up to its big brother China, with its back to Laos and Thailand and its rump nudging Cambodia. Its eye

1 Rush hour in Saigon. **2** Squid fishers on Phan Thiet. **3** Bad luck for lucky birds. **4** Flower power in Chau Doc. **5** Off to the highlands.

is the capital Hanoi, its nose is Haiphong. The slim neck extends from Vinh to Quy Nhon, and the paunch curves across Ho Chi Minh City into the Mekong Delta, the tip of which could be the tail. Patriotic Vietnamese prefer to interpret the shape as depicting their traditional bamboo yoke with rice baskets suspended at each end, an image which symbolizes the equilibrium between the two deltas – the Mekong in the south and the Red River Delta in the north. However, critical compatriots offer a more modern interpretation, comparing the outline of their country to a dollar sign. An audacious view, but not a prohibited one in a Communist country which is currently experiencing such a rapid economic boom that many are growing concerned about its future. The country is facing a greater transformation than ever before in its short history of

1 2

peace. No war has succeeded in bringing about such far-reaching changes as Doi Moi, the capitalist tightrope walk of Vietnam's Communist Party. A tightrope suspended between socialism and capitalism, where the walk is done to a Western tune and the bar is set at a lofty height. Too high, say many, pointing to the identity crisis into which the country is inevitably plunged when progress is controlled from outside – with the money of foreign investors whose only concern in this development is to turn a quick profit. In the giant strides Vietnam is taking to catch up with Asia's "tiger" economies, preservation of its traditions is both the country's most important and most sensitive task, for the Vietnamese – despite their highly future-oriented way of life – hold a canon of deeply mystical beliefs which have shaped their culture over the centuries. Their greatest source of strength is derived from the world of their spirits and ancestors. If the equilibrium of these traditional values is disrupted, the country will lose its lovable, enigmatic soul.

In a timely response, many hotel chains are now taking countermeasures against the architectural eyesores and ecological atrocities of the first boom. A critical factor of these new projects is their integration into existing structures such as agricultural systems and village environments, creating employment and opening up new markets for the rural population. Examples include the Life Resort at Quy Nhon, "Cassias Cottage" on Phu Quoc, and Eco-Lodges in the far north. These realistic models are based on the principle of Taoism, a set of teachings dating back to the 7th century BC which calls for a return to nature and which seeks the "Great Way," or dao, in which all things flow in harmony. Whether chosen consciously or unconsciously, this way generates respect in people into whose personal environment one introduces change, enabling all parties to keep their countenance. In Vietnam this is a key precondition for harmonious coexistence, playing a vital role in everyday life. Foreign eyes may fail to perceive this harmony, believing the very idea of harmony to be an absurdity in the face of Vietnam's day-to-day chaos. And yet it is unwise to underestimate the Vietnamese for this reason.

Vietnam's history tells many a tale of kings and generals who, although despised by their powerful, arrogant opponents, applied crafty battle strategies and eventually triumphed over their enemies. Take King Le Loi, for example, who used a trick to destroy the Chinese fleet, or the Hai Ba Trung sisters, the most courageous women ever to lead an army. Their names are still featured on many street signs today.

In the country's more recent history, the victories against French and US troops at Dien Bien Phu and Saigon have become the basis of a cautious form of propaganda. The War Crimes Museum was recently renamed and is now known as The War Remnants Museum.

To understand Vietnam more deeply, it is well worth while to browse through its history in the many outstanding museums throughout the country. Hanoi is also home to a Women's Museum, portraying the role of women in Vietnam's modern wars in straightforward exhibitions of political correctness and objectivity, which are perhaps all the more horrifying for that reason. By this point at the latest, we can grasp the conviction and strength with which the country fought for its freedom. Many US American visitors from the generation of war veterans leave the museum shamefaced and stricken, perhaps having only now discovered that they were fighting against women who were invincible.

The invincibility of women continues to this day in a more modern form in Vietnam's international business life. Many a "proud peacock" with a briefcase and sharply pressed pants has embarked on negotiations with a Vietnamese businesswoman only to find his feathers flying during the opening round of talks, and wished himself safe in a gathering of men negotiating over rice wine – or even back in his homeland. A gilded statue of "Mother Vietnam" occupies its rightful place in the Hanoi Women's Museum. Towering lifesize over the entrance and holding a child in her arms she is impossible to ignore. Sea horses, dollar signs, yokes with rice baskets – whatever images we may choose to compare Vietnam's geographical outlines, the geography of the country is easy to remember.

1 Cham temple towers at Po Nagar. **2** Jungle pool at Evason Hideaway. **3** Tam Thai Pagoda on the "marble mountain" Thuy Son. **4** Temple of the Japanese Bridge at Hoi An.

The laziest simply divide the country neatly through the middle into south and north along the 17th parallel, which played such a significant role in the last war as the Demilitarized Zone. A more detailed approach is to divide the country into South, North, and Central Vietnam to create a clearer picture. However, to gain the most informative impression of Vietnam's geographical diversity, I recommend memorizing the following regions from south to north: the Mekong Delta (Can Tho), the southeast (Ho Chi Minh City), the central uplands (Dalat), the southern (Hoi An) and northern (Vinh) Central Coast, the Red River Delta (Hanoi), the northwest (Sapa) and the northeast (Lao Cai). Now the scope of Vietnam's geographical variety begins to emerge. The elongated country, a mere 50 kilometers (30 miles) wide in the province of Quang Binh, also has a few surprises to offer with regard to its weather. The Vietnamese say that it's always raining somewhere, or it's too hot or too cold. Well, their country does lie in a tropical monsoon region which has only two seasons: the rainy season from May to October and the dry period from November to April. However, this is somewhat oversimplified: the north has two additional transitional seasons which may bring fog, dampness, and

1 Crafts displayed at the market. **2** Influx from the mountains – Bac Ha Sunday market. **3** Sailing with dragons in Halong Bay. **4** to **7** Le Van Dung prepares a Vietnamese noodle soup.

even snow. As a rule of thumb, the months from October to March are considered the best for traveling, depending, of course, on the type of vacation travelers seek. Vietnam, which first began to welcome tourists a mere thirteen years ago, now offers everything from adventure trips to swimming, luxury or spa vacations, or even rugged hiking tours.

Mountains or valleys, water or woods, beach or city – Hanoi or Ho Chi Minh City? It's like trying to decide between operetta or opera, Woodstock or La Scala in Milan. Life in the metropolis of Hanoi is different from the megacity of Ho Chi Minh.

Hanoi is cozier, easier to navigate, more down-to-earth and genuine than its way-out sister in the South, which is still described as the most charming city in Asia. In this context, it is also referred to as Saigon – not so off the mark, for the airport code is SGN and not HCMC, as the younger generation flippantly, and slightly disrespectfully, refer to the city, even though the first district, the city center and location of most of the grand hotels, is actually called Saigon.

However, both cities, Hanoi and Ho Chi Minh City, are absolutely typical of Vietnam; the variations in lifestyle quite simply correlate to the variety of mentalities to be found between north and south. A nice example to illustrate this north-south divide, which one also finds in other countries, is Germany's lovingly tended "love-hate relationship" between the "Prussians" in the north of the country and the Bavarians in the south – completely superfluous, of course, but generally a source of amusement. In fact, the North Vietnamese are often known as the "Prussians of Asia" for their punctuality and reliability, throwing an even clearer light on the differences. However, it is ultimately irrelevant how travelers plan, begin or end their journey to Vietnam; they simply cannot go wrong, provided they avoid any attempt to cram in a succession of exhausting tours with the aim of seeing everything at once and getting to know a little of everything. Our journey of discovery through Vietnam should, therefore, be viewed not as a complete travel guide from A to Z, but as an in-depth examination of a country and its people, whose wit and charm are endlessly fascinating – a country which has veiled its old wounds in new magic, and which despite, or perhaps even because of, its painful scars now looks to a peaceful future. Ho Chi Minh City is the starting point of this journey between the past and the present. A city that is exciting, inspiring,

baffling, and irritating by turns, and whose heart still bears the melodious name of its former golden age: Saigon.
From this new megacity, which unofficial estimates claim has already exceeded the 10-million mark, the journey continues to the Mekong Delta, Vietnam's "rice bowl" region and lifeline. After exploring Saigon and drinking in the overwhelming impressions of the Mekong Delta, we discover tranquility and deserted beaches on the island paradise of Phu Quoc, in Vietnam's southwest. We then travel from jungle and beach over the mountains to the sea, crossing the southern uplands to the south coast: Dalat, Mui Ne, Na Trang, idyllic bathing resorts with the flair of the Caribbean. In Central Vietnam the ancient port of Hoi An and the imperial city of Hue beckon with charming laneways, old merchants' houses, and a millennium of history. From the capital, Hanoi, that austere northern beauty, we enter mysterious Halong Bay and cross the mountains to Sapa, 1,600 meters (5,248 feet) above sea level.
At weekends, the bustling, vibrant markets are thronged with colorfully dressed mountain peoples from the surrounding regions who meet to offer their wares. The enormous diversity in the costumes, dialects, and customs of these ethnic minorities clearly indicate that Vietnam must master many challenges spanning tradition and progress on its way into the future.

At the end of the journey we return to Hanoi, that venerable lady of somber charm, either to fly home or, for those beginning their journey in the north, to continue their travels to the south. Travelers on the night train from Lao Cai to the Chinese border arrive thoroughly shaken up in Hanoi the next morning. Taking the day train is little better. However, although Vietnam is not a country for train travel, we should brave the tracks just once for a small adventure. Our travels will leave us rich in experiences and discoveries which are almost impossible to make in other countries, in a country we fear because of the firmly rooted images in our memories which have shaped an entire generation. Now, our encounters with the people in this country, its culture, and natural beauty have wiped out the terrible pictures from the past, leaving our valuable and enduring memories of the journey.

Sated with happiness

Sated with happiness – for the Vietnamese, this state means a laden table, steaming bowls of rice, meat, fish, and plenty of vegetables, all, of course, freshly picked and deliciously crisp. Eating and drinking are the pinnacle of life to the Vietnamese, who enjoy assembling in large gatherings to share this philosophy. Don't miss an opportunity to join them – there's no better way to get to know Vietnam.
Vietnamese cuisine is still regarded as natural and traditional, owing to the traditional methods with which most of the ingredients are prepared. However, the fusion of Asian and French cuisine has created a new culinary style which tests the limits of some chefs. But the plates are soon cleared and we can look forward to the next *pho bo*, the simple Vietnamese noodle soup with beef, or the "Da Nang Flat Noodle" from Central Vietnam, prepared by head chef Le Van Dung from the Life Resort Hoi An.

Ingredients: 300 grams chicken, 200 grams ribbon noodles, 50 grams tomatoes, 50 grams onions, 25 grams pineapple, 1 prawn cracker, 10 grams peanuts, mixed seasonal herbs, salt, pepper, lime juice, and chili.
Braise the chicken, sauté the vegetables and noodles, season to taste, and serve with a crispy rice-paper spring roll, peanuts, and sesame crackers.

MINH MUÔN

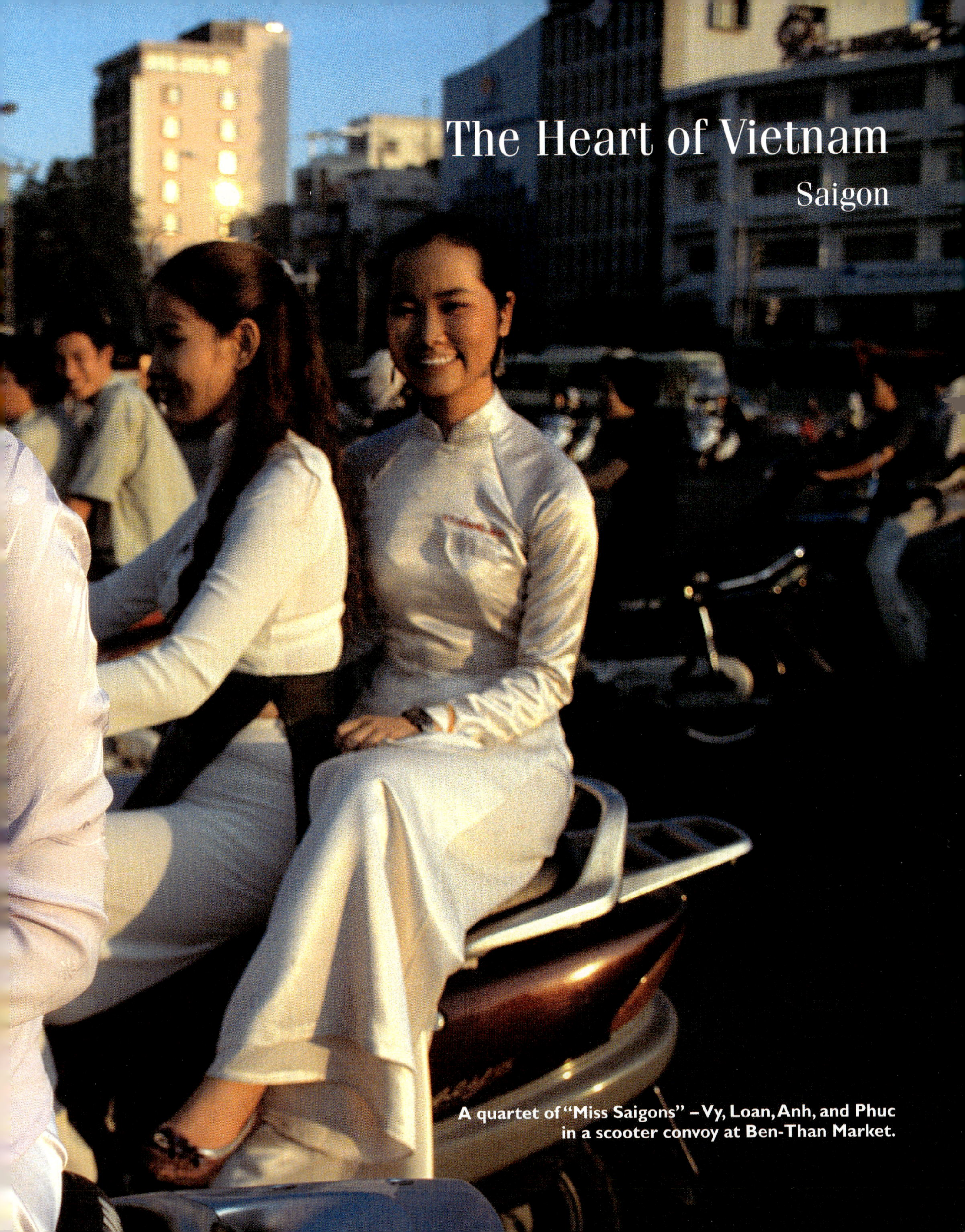

The Heart of Vietnam

Saigon

A quartet of "Miss Saigons" – Vy, Loan, Anh, and Phuc in a scooter convoy at Ben-Than Market.

HSBC

Ancient Glory Under a New Name

The Heart of Vietnam – Ho Chi Minh City

A popular Vietnamese proverb claims "Imperial law stops at the village hedge" – or at the boundary of Ho Chi Minh City.

The modern version of this ancient saying expresses a philosophy which is characteristic of the people in this city, and which sums up their attitude to life: Saigon has always been a law unto itself. Like a younger sister who stubbornly retains her wildness, despite the conservative attempts of her older sister Hanoi to teach her manners.

It's this attitude that makes Vietnam's largest city so attractive and full of flair. Saigon is the perfect setting for a plot that's a combination of "dancing on a volcano" and anarchy. And yet the mixture is anything but abhorrent.

As soon as the shock of arrival has given way to fascination, the lungs have grown accustomed to the overdose of exhaust fumes, and the ears to the permanent cacophony of car horns, we notice how much friendliness there is here in this sprawling megacity. Like Vietnam's wonderful national dish, the firepot fondue known as *lau*, the bubbling melting pot that is Saigon is crammed with all kinds of ingredients from daily life. *Lau* contains every kind of produce Vietnam has to offer: herbs, spices and vegetables, meat or fish. Anyone can help to prepare it and watch fascinated as it simmers. The end result is unique and supremely delicious. And discovering Saigon is like the first taste of *lau* – too spicy, too hot, too much or too little, too loud or too quiet. But it's never wrong – it's all a question of taste.

After taking their first hesitant steps, travelers will be quick to assemble their own personal stew of fascinating impressions. The perfect way to do this is to stroll through District 1, between the Saigon River in the east and the cathedral of Notre Dame, next to the fabulous main post office, in the west. Streets in this district follow a grid pattern, and all explorers need to do is to remember the direction they came from. The diversity of the buildings, spanning French colonial architecture, colossal modern towers of glass and steel, and quaint, narrow Vietnamese houses, creates an impression of how the city has constantly adjusted to different eras under new rulers throughout the course of its history, yet has

1 Cyclo in Rue Pasteur. **2** Cellphone mania extends to cafés.
3 Stradivarius? Anything's possible in the markets of the historic quarter.
4 Old Notre-Dame in modern company.

succeeded in retaining its own identity. That must be why the city and its inhabitants are so calm when faced with the dawn of yet another new era – it's their adaptability and their unique blend of Eurasian charm. Miss Saigon, the legendary name applied to the delicate Vietnamese women in their silk *ao dai* dresses, is the most vibrant symbol of this powerful charisma, unrivaled in her beauty and grace, admired by women, and worshiped by men. To the latter, however, she is more generally a source of pain. While not unapproachable, she remains unattainable for the majority, a tragic situation addressed by many novels – although today's Saigonese male would commit such literary suffering to paper in the form of a melancholy true-life report, particularly while watching the crowds of *ao dai*-clad girls strolling down the famous Dong Khoi promenade.

Staring at the traffic is the only effective distraction. Saigon's roads are ruled by two-wheelers – or to be precise, one-handers, since cyclists generally use one of their hands to carry something. Usually

5

6

1 The world's most beautiful post office. **2** A postmark from Saigon is a nice souvenir. **3** Art Déco in Saigon on the Majestic's roof terrace. **4** Saigon striving upwards. **5** City oasis – the pool at the Majestic. **6** Fresh towels.

1

2

it's a cell phone; occasionally the "spare" hand is used to steady the wobbling cargo or hold onto a chic hat. A moped can easily accommodate two passengers, although three are a squeeze; occasionally, families of five squash together and plunge, sitting, standing or crouching on their tiny, pestilential two-stroke machines, into the hurly-burly of the evening metropolis. The Misses Saigon often ride pillion sidesaddle, sometimes even wearing an *ao dai* but preferably in skintight jeans. These jaunty scooter girls show no signs of female insecurity in this parade of two-wheelers; they have long since won the respect of their fellow road users the hard way with their brisk, confident style. However, their smiles are generally hidden; elegant Vietnamese women avoid sunshine, for a tan is the country bumpkin's badge of poverty and is shunned by city dwellers, who favor a distinguished pallor. They protect themselves from the sun by wearing gloves to the elbow, racy hats, and big face masks. Not a very effective crumple zone, but who cares? In fact, a surprisingly low number of accidents take place in the city, at the average speed of 30 to 40 kilometers (18 to 24 miles) per hour and a strictly observed highway code. Rule number one: Wherever you find a space, move into it. Rule number two: Might is right. And rule number three: Right of way belongs to whoever's ahead. When these rules are followed considerately, it's easy to grasp the secret of Vietnamese traffic, which screeches to a halt for only one reason: a bewildered foreign pedestrian suddenly stopping dead in the midst of the hubbub. This inevitably leads to disarray on the city's streets. Saigon is designed for movement, mobility, and making headway.

Because order must reign in the midst of chaos, the city is divided into nineteen districts plus five rural districts. All are numbered, and the numbers are displayed clearly on the houses, giving the "HCMC" novice the courage to undertake further expeditions. For example, a visit to the restaurant Quan An Ngon in District One. Twenty chefs, each a master of a different Vietnamese specialty, regale their guests on the restaurant's four floors. A good place to make the acquaintance of the classic noodle soup *pho bo*, spring rolls, and other classics of Vietnamese cuisine. Fertilized duck eggs, the first stop on the culinary expedition, are not essential.

Also in District One or Saigon proper is the Palace of Reunification. On April 30, 1975, a North Vietnamese soldier hoisted the

Vietcong flag on its balcony as a sign of victory over the capitalist superpower America, the land of opportunity. Today, however, it is Communist Ho Chi Minh City which is the "city of opportunity," attracting billions of dollars in investments from the former opponents and enemies of the people.

War, victory, and the suffering caused by war are topics which can scarcely be avoided in Vietnam unless one decides to completely ignore this chapter of Vietnamese history. The Vietnamese themselves do not hanker after discussions on the topic; questions concerning the war are answered politely but impassively. No complaints about the past are heard – those times were hard enough. Now the people are determined to look eagerly into the future. "Ahead of us lies the future, and that's all we are able to shape," say the old people. And the younger ones are keen to plunge into the glittering world of temptations they have experienced only from television. Around 40 percent of Vietnam's population is aged under 30. It's easy to understand that young people are occasionally amused, but more often irritated, when yet another tourist asks "Which way to the war?

1 Times are lousy in the old quarter. **2** Found in every travel guide – Nguyen Hue traffic circle. **3** High-tech cyclo for a glittering city. **4** Chinese chess on the sidewalk. **5** Everyday routine.

1 Any time of day – incense for the ancestors. 2 A cage of temple sparrows. 3 Courtyard of Thien Hau Pagoda, dedicated to the goddess of fishermen and sailors. 4 Temple of the Jade Emperor. 5 The monk calms the Horse of Death with his bell. 6 Offering prayers for the baby is a Vietnamese tradition.

Ho Chi Minh City houses an array of museums which offer insights into the Vietnam War. The War Remnants Museum, formerly named War Crimes Museum, primarily examines the "American War," as the last war is known to the Vietnamese. In its forecourt stand exhibits of bombs, helicopters, and aircraft; inside, horror awaits. Oversized photographs familiar from news broadcasts. Images one would have preferred to forget now become newly awakened memories for visitors to a country they yearn to visit in peace. Many emerge from the museum in tears, some leave immediately they see the hall of photos. But for the Vietnamese, these museums are a top priority – as sources of revenue. The War Remnants Museum registers the highest number of visitors in the city.

The city's Art Museum is a more peaceful location. The exhibits of political art, depicting scenes of war in heroic images, are almost

refreshing after the war photographs. But they, too, can be avoided by an orderly retreat to the second floor. The gilded Buddhas and statues of the Cham people exhibited here are considered to be among the finest in the country. Fortunately, the route from the museums into the pulsating life of the city is not long. Pho Duc Chinh Street leads directly to the main entrance of Ben Than Market, with its enormous clock face, which actually makes it look like a railway station. But what's on the label isn't always inside, and not even the longest description could do justice to what's inside here. In a nutshell, it's the city's liveliest trading center, over a century old. You'll miss most of it if you remain under the shady roof of the former Halles Centrales: the most entertaining traders are found outside on the crammed sidewalks. They shouldn't actually be here at all, so they are under enormous creative pressure to come up with sales pitches before the police move them on again.

Cholon is a mysterious, secretive, enigmatic name, and this impression remains even after we discover that it means nothing more arcane than "Great Market." The inscrutable Chinese heart of the Vietnamese city, with its nightmarish legends of opium dens and dens of vice, beats less strongly for visitors from a foreign world than for its own kind, but the little it reveals of its throbbing life is thrilling enough.

Here, in District Five only seven kilometers (4 miles) away from the center, time seems to have stood still. Binh Tay Market, under the mighty roof of a decaying market hall, stocks everything Asian hearts desire. Here, traditional trading methods have the upper hand over prosperity and progress. Tourists are amazed. Everything that is definitely superfluous on a journey beckons to you to buy it. Food stalls serving delicious soups and rice dishes are a seductive siren call to ignore the principles of survival which travelers have brought from home: "Never eat at markets, never drink juice from street stands, and always boil water." Actually, the greatest danger is quite different: insidious, silent, from below. It's those little plastic chairs that gradually collapse under the weight of European bodies. First slowly, then faster, until a "crack" is heard, a burst of laughter rises, a fresh bowl of soup is poured by the giggling cook and two new chairs are produced – stacked on top of each other to provide more stability.

See page 25

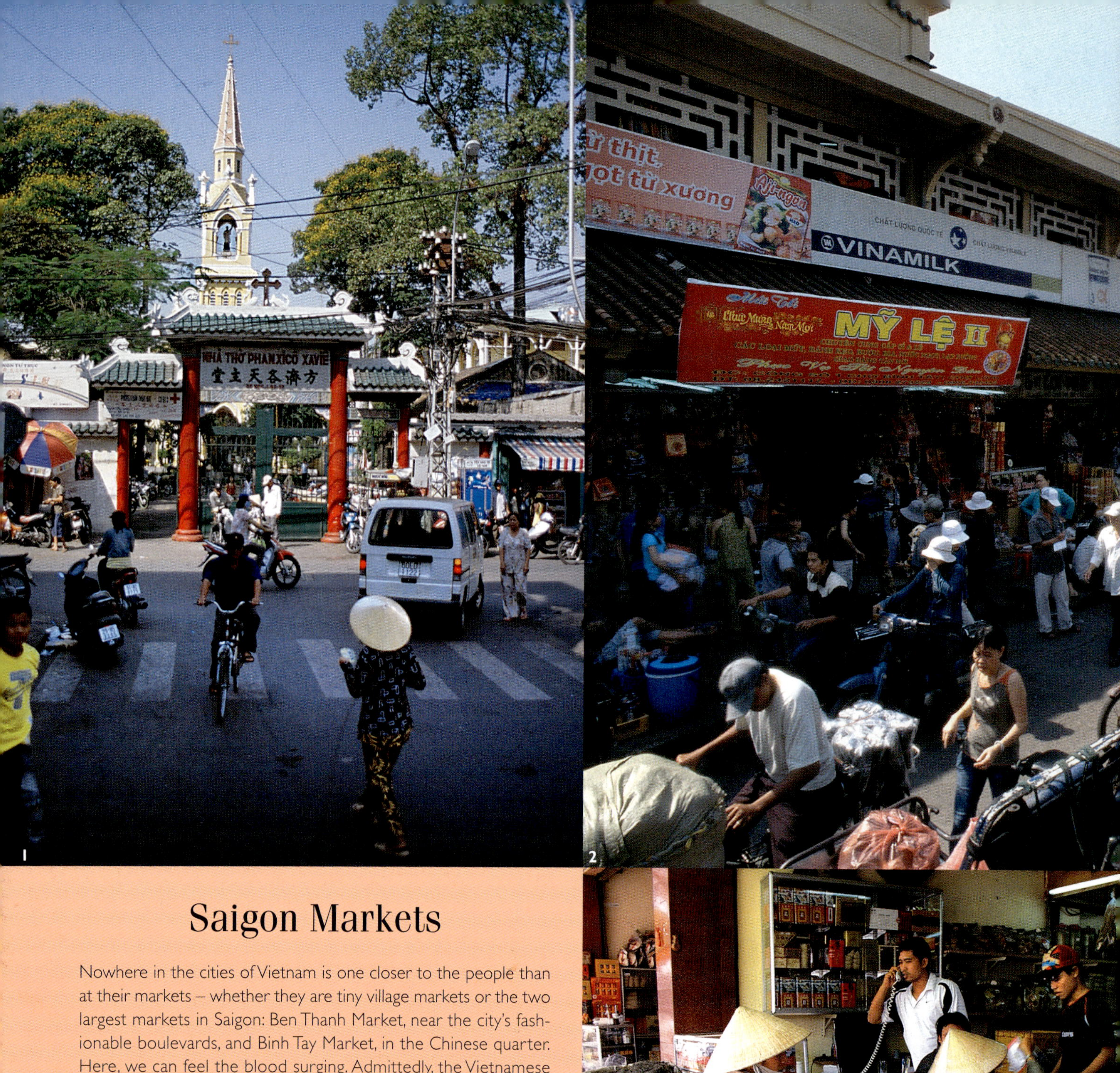

Saigon Markets

Nowhere in the cities of Vietnam is one closer to the people than at their markets – whether they are tiny village markets or the two largest markets in Saigon: Ben Thanh Market, near the city's fashionable boulevards, and Binh Tay Market, in the Chinese quarter. Here, we can feel the blood surging. Admittedly, the Vietnamese love trading of all kinds, but the act of trading may often take on enhanced significance as a first-class source of communication and news. No one pays any attention to the tourists – life goes on as it always has done. Sometimes we "long-noses" ourselves become newsworthy, when our behavior or appearance inspires witty comments.

1 Harmony of religions – Cholon. **2** Binh Tay Market – Saigon's Chinatown. **3** Ben Than Market, main gate. **4** Street of medicinal herbs, Cholon. **5** The best food is found where the Vietnamese themselves eat. **6** Get ahead with a hat – the agony of choice.

CHỢ BẾN THÀNH
3
6

1

2

3

4

1 In peace lies strength – rush hour in Saigon. **2** Protecting the skin – the upper classes wear white. **3** Fido comes, too – mopeds transport everything. **4** "Drive in" for strawberries – life on the move in Saigon. **5** Lunch break for the soul – L'Apothiquaire temple of health. **6** Pool life amid the city. **7** Relaxing between meetings.

And if a bruise remains, don't worry. The Chinese pharmacies and herb stores opposite stock ointments, tinctures, and mysterious liquids to cure all aches and pains. The sight of the colorful plants, knotted roots, and fragrant powders alone befuddles the senses from afar. Any ailment can be treated here. Ingredients are freshly ground, crushed, and mixed in front of the patient's eyes. "Long-noses" are given painstaking advice: trust engenders loyalty among customers. Hypochondriacs have their own department, in the stores that stock pickled frogs, cobras, spiders, and lizards. A salubrious sight. It only remains to test the effect of these animal concentrates on potency or to see the Chinese doctor straightaway. His methods of diagnosis may be surprising, but they are based on an eminently credible foundation: "A skilful doctor treats the healthy, a bad doctor treats the sick," say the Chinese. They measure a doctor's skill by the number of healthy patients he has, not by the crowds in his waiting-room, as we Europeans do. The doctor's fee depends on the population's state of health. He earns the most when he has nothing to do. It's no wonder that accurate diagnosis is the linchpin of his art: diagnosis by examining the tongue or eyes, diagnosis by smell. The doctor devises a course of personalized treatment on the basis of his findings. Many a Westerner has left a doctor's practice in the Chinese quarter completely speechless, with the beginnings of a new broad-mindedness dawning that enhance his perception of the Vietnamese rituals of well-being.

Young and old affectionately honor their gods in magnificent temples and pagodas. Thien Hau Pagoda in Cholon, dedicated to the Chinese sea goddess, and the Temple of the Jade Emperor in the northeast of Saigon are among the most beautiful jewels of religious culture in Saigon. Incense sticks and gently tinkling bells not only calm the Jade Emperor's horse of death, but also soothe our nerves. Calmness is strength, so that it may be useful to seek other methods of fighting the wave of nervousness, the jetlag, and the hot flushes caused by the abrupt change in climate. Perhaps a famous Vietnamese massage? There's something

1 Evening view of Hotel Majestic. **2** The lobby of the Majestic – 100 years of history. **3** Park Hyatt Hotel – Saigon's "Number One". **4** A fantastic reception in the Park Hyatt. **5** Food with a view – cooking tableside. **6** Park Hyatt, elegant rooms.

for everyone, from head to toe. "Sinful Saigon" offers the most comprehensive range of serious massages anywhere in Vietnam. Foot massages are available from the shoeshine boy, head massages from the barber, hand massages from the manicurist. It seems to be a national pastime. But don't overdo it in the first few days; the action of these powerful hands can result in aching muscles. It's wiser to visit specialist masseurs and spa staff. The major hotels such as Park Hyatt, Majestic, Caravelle, and Rex are well equipped, extending their top-class service to non-residents, too. However, there are also insiders' tips offering an elegance, comfort, and atmosphere unequalled by any hotel. Many go there to recover from the day's experiences and gather strength for an exciting night.

Ho Chi Minh City – Saigon, the city of contrasts. By day, the ravenous maws of the demolition diggers devour shaky colonial houses, while by night these remaining witnesses to the past are bathed in warm light as if to apologize, interspersed by flashing neon signs exuding their seductive capitalist charm. Even the garish blue neon of the little stores on Le Loi between the opera house square and Ben Than Market create a cheerful, friendly mood, a mellow protection against the permanent barrage of "Hey, Mister" hustlers. There is no patent recipe against these annoying creatures. And unless you really want a copy of the latest literary best seller as an original pirate copy for two dollars, simply keep walking and try to shut your ears.

Rescue awaits at the end of the magnificent boulevard, at the main gate of Ben Than Market. The cyclo driver who saves me just happens to have time to show me the rest of the city on my way back to the hotel – which is, actually, only a short ride away. There is no patent remedy against this either; we have to accept

that the driver really needs the money, which in turn is our chance to save him. Celebrate in the new Park Hyatt on Lam Son Square, the most prestigious address in the center of Saigon. Despite its enormous size, the lobby has a welcoming, almost cozy atmosphere, offering cosmopolitan flair at its most charming and the finest coffee and cake in the city. Glorious Saigon is more real in these surroundings than in many a state-run hotel.

Some 200 meters (660 feet) further, the terrace of the venerable Continental, where Graham Greene wrote his novel *The Quiet American*, is the perfect spot for a pleasant evening. From here we can survey the Opera, Le Loi boulevard, and the new Caravelle, built adjacent to the old hotel. The older wing is almost invisible as it clings to the modern building, as if seeking protection from the new age. Once the first choice for war correspondents from all over the world, today the hotel is history. The terrace of the Saigon Bar on the 10th floor was a "watch-tower of war," and many a reporter scribbled his bulletins about the advancing Vietcong here while clutching a Scotch or brandy, red wine or beer, depending on his nationality. Today, the terrace still offers newsworthy sights, with the most magnificent view of the city by night.

The roof garden of the Rex has a similar history. This was the information center of the US press officers; today, guests can listen to live music and gaze at the most frequently photographed traffic circle in the world, without which no magazine or book on Vietnam would be complete.

The Majestic, once the most elegant hotel in Saigon, offers a superb view across the broad Saigon River, the ideal spot to watch the lantern-festooned dinner junks glide past while sipping a sundowner. This is an excellent place to let one's mind wander in peace; here, the roar of the traffic comes from one side only, dropping to a whisper and slipping out of the city on the waters of the long, quiet river. The river unloads it, together with the bad

news of the day, somewhere out in the ocean. Life is like a river, say the Vietnamese; the source constantly supplies fresh vigor – and they ensure they are fit for it every day.

It's a regular morning sight. As soon as the sun rises, an inexorable tide of people begins to move. In Van Hoa Park behind the Palace of Reunification, on sidewalks, on the riverbank, the same ritual takes place everywhere: the Vietnamese practice traditional tai chi, Asian meditation, and Western jogging to bring body and soul into harmony and prepare them for the stress of the city and for new challenges.

1 Continental, Saigon's oldest hotel. **2** Children's play area in the foyer of Hotel Caravelle. **3** Disneyland in Saigon, Hotel Caravelle. **4** Miss Saigon asks for the pleasure. **5** Quan An Ngon, Saigon's finest eating house. **6** The team at Exotissimo Saigon: Pantanida Jantsakool, Richard Craik, Olivier Colomès.

Ho Chi Minh City – new name, ancient glory

What to see
Palace of Reunification, War Remnants Museum, National Art Museum, Ben Thanh Market, Cholon, Binh Tay Market, Thien Hau Pagoda, Temple of the Jade Emperor

Where to stay
Park Hyatt Saigon, 2 Lam Son Square, Tel: 0084-88241234, e-mail: saigon.park@hyattintl.com, www.saigon.park.hyatt.com. Park Hyatt is the most comfortable hotel in Saigon's center.
Majestic Hotel, 1 Dong Khoi St. Tel: 0084-88295517, e-mail: majestic@majesticsaigon.com.vn, www.majesticsaigon.com.vn.
Attractive hotel with colonial façade and elegant foyer.
Hotel Continental, 132–134 Dong Khoi St.; Graham Greene wrote his novel *The Quiet American* here. Both the hotel and the novel are still legendary.
Tel: 0084-88299201, e-mail: continental@hcm.vnn.vn, www.continental-saigon.com.vn.
Hotel Caravelle, 19 Lam Son Square. Tel: 0084-88234999, e-mail: hotel@caravellehotel.vnn.vn, www.caravellehotel.com.
Rex Hotel, 141 Nguyen Hue Blvd. Tel: 0084-88292185 or: 0084-88293115, e-mail: rexhotel@hcm.vnn.vn, www.rexhotelvietnam.com

Where to eat and drink
The perfect place for a sundowner is the bar of the *Majestic Hotel*. The best coffee and cake can be found in the spacious foyer of the *Park Hyatt*.

6

Special recommendations
Stroll through colonial Saigon along Dong Khoi
Fitness for the soul, La Maison de L'Apothiquaire, 64A Truong Dinh St. Tel: 0084-89325181, www.lapothiquaire.com
Fitness for the camera: Vietnam's best camera specialist, Mr. Anh Tuan, 11 Le Cong Kieu St. Tel.: 0084-8295888, e-mail: phamthe11@hcm.vnn.vn

Information
Exotissimo Travel Vietnam Co Ltd, Saigon Finance Center 9 Dinh Tien Hoang, District 1, *Ho Chi Minh City.*
Tel: 0084-88251723-283,
e-mail: infoEXO@exotissimo.com,
go.vietnam@exotissimo.com,
www.exotissimo.com

Cao Daism, Attempting to Create a Universal Religion

Tay Ninh – Home of the Religions

*"Because of the very multiplicity of religions,
humanity cannot always live in harmony.
That is why I decided to unite all these religions into one
to bring them back to the primordial unity."*

These words were announced in the 1920s by a forty-something Vietnamese civil servant in the French colonial government. Ngo Van Chieu had presided over numerous séances, where he experienced impressive apparitions of a Supreme Being, Cao Dai, amassing 247 followers of his revelations in the process. He felt a vocation to unite the teachings of the founders of Western and Eastern religions, to bring them together under a single roof, in a universal religion focused on a universal God – from Confucius, Buddha, and Jesus Christ to Mohammed.

Funded by private donations, the largest temple of the rapidly growing Cao Dai sect was built in Tay Ninh as early as 1933, and is still the headquarters of Caodaism. Cao Dai's hierarchical structure is similar to that of Roman Catholicism. A Pope, cardinals, bishops, and priests congregate at the Holy See in the Holy City on the periphery of Tay Ninh. The compound is practically a mini-Vatican, functioning along similar lines to its more famous model. However, the "job" of Pope is currently vacant, and Caodaism has experienced only one Pope. Caodaism is the third most prevalent religion in Vietnam after Buddhism and Catholicism.

Caodaism is believed to have around 30,000 followers in the USA, Europe, and Australia. The religion's main principles focus on reincarnation, prohibition of alcohol, selflessness, non-violence. Charity and poverty are regarded as moral obligations.

The pantheon of Cao Dai "saints" has integrated – unbidden – such illustrious names as Victor Hugo, Joan of Arc, and Isaac Newton. Communication with these luminaries can be established as required by means of special messages, in which their precious teachings are preserved for humanity.

The former civil servant and founder of the religion, Ngo Van Chieu, soon found himself in favor not only with the holy spirits and their universal God, but also with the French colonial government. The new religion was officially recognized as early as 1926, and developed considerable political potential. In the 1950s, the

1 and **3** Awaiting the crowds of tourists, nuns, and high priests.
2 The Divine Eye is all-seeing. **4** The blue throne of Cao Dai, center of the religion.

1 Paying respects to the Divine Eye. **2** and **3** Noonday worship – priests and nuns. **4** Barefoot into the temple – the holy marble floors may not be defiled with shoes.

Caodaists established a private army of 50,000 troops to protect themselves. "The teachings of Moses are the bud, the teachings of Christ are the flower, and Cao Dai is the fruit."

The Communists took a different view, closing the temple in 1975 and packing its priests off for reeducation. Since 1990, Vietnam's traditional religious tolerance has again reasserted itself and the temples are now open to all, resuming their teaching of wisdom, tolerance, and humanity as preached by Confucius, Buddha, Jesus Christ, and Mohammed. The principle of uniting all religions under a universal God in human form, however, is no longer included in the teachings, being too great a cause of unrest. A final revelation delivered the solution to this all-too-human problem: the Supreme Being appeared only as a divine light, now installed on a glittering globe as an all-seeing "Divine Eye." The feeling is clear: this magic eye is truly omnispective.

Many visitors, however, are cowed in its presence. Even though the globe is, fortunately, in semi-darkness at the front of the temple, its stern gaze conveys a merciless warning. Cameras remain in

pockets, shoes are obediently taken off at the entrance. The midday service is more relaxed.

The colorful procession, held every day at noon on the dot, attracts crowds of spectators. Most have traveled from Ho Chi Minh City, a distance of 90 kilometers (ca. 50 miles), to Tay Ninh in the upper Mekong Delta, a mere 26 kilometers (ca. 16 miles) from the Cambodian border. It is often a tiring journey that may take at least three hours, and so it is useful to combine it with a visit to the tunnel of Cu Chi – a practical plan which is a mixed blessing, not only because of the contrasting aspects of war and religion, but also because of the departure time: 5 a.m. from Ho Chi Minh City. However, the visit is well worth while. Enormous crowds gather at the Cao Dai temple, and latecomers must stay outside when worship begins – a torment for photography fans. The service begins with a procession of worshippers in three lines. Men file over to the right and center of the temple, while women take their places on the left. All kneel and bow three times, spreading a sea of colorful robes over the gleaming tiled floor of the gigantic temple. Red robes signify adherents of Confucius, while saffron yellow is worn by Buddhists, and blue by Taoists. White is considered the symbol of purity and may be worn by all.

Tay Ninh – home of the religions

What to see

Visit the noontime *Cao Dai service* at Tay Ninh. If you are interested in the tunnel system used by the Vietcong, combine your visit to the temple with a tour of *Cu Chi*, located halfway between Saigon and Tay Ninh.

Where to stay

Tay Ninh is a day excursion from Saigon. See page 29.

Where to eat and drink

There are no recommended restaurants in the vicinity of the temple. However, between *Cu Chi* and *Tay Ninh* there are numerous small restaurants which are worth a visit despite being located on a main tourist route.

Special recommendation

The temple is one of the most popular subjects for photographers in the whole of Vietnam, and is naturally famous. Photography fans should go early to secure the most discreet places on the balustrade next to the novices' chambers, to the left and right of the gallery. Don't forget your tripod, and don't use flash: in the unaccustomed color and brightness of the temple, it's easy to forget that it is a place of worship.

Information

Asia Explorer, 87 Nghia Thuc St., Tel: 0084-82123133
or: 9242092, fax: 0084-89242093,
e-mail: asia-explore@vnn.vn,
www.asia-explorer.vn

Exotissimo Travel Vietnam Co Ltd, Saigon Finance Center
9 Dinh Tien Hoang, District 1, *Ho Chi Minh City.*
Tel: 0084-88251723-283,
e-mail: infoEXO@exotissimo.com,
go.vietnam@exotissimo.com,
www.exotissimo.com

Cai Rang, where everything's afloat: houses, vegetables, melons ...

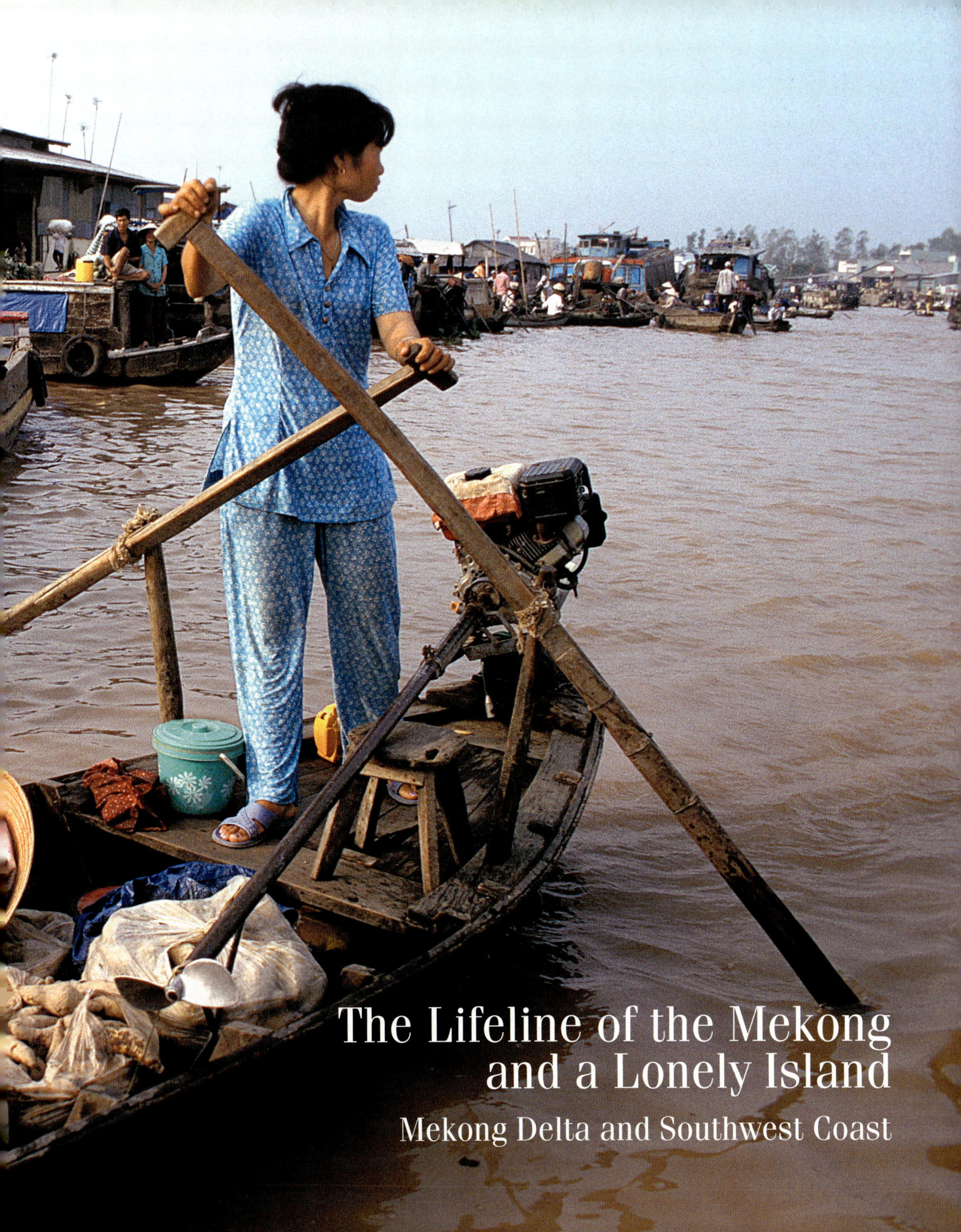

The Lifeline of the Mekong and a Lonely Island

Mekong Delta and Southwest Coast

"The Mother of All Waters"

The Mekong as Lifeline

A Vietnamese proverb runs,
"When you drink water, think of its source."
While that makes sense to most people,
the source of the Mekong was shrouded in mystery for centuries.

One of the last great mysteries of the world was not solved until well into the 1990s. It is now known that the source of "the Mother of All Rivers" is in the Tibetan Plateau, in the remote region known as the Roof of the World. By the time that the brown waters of the Mekong reach the estuary below Saigon on the Yellow Sea and spill into the delta like a vast fan, they have passed through five countries – China, Myanmar (Burma), Laos, Thailand, and Cambodia – and covered around 4,800 kilometers (2,880 miles).

The Mekong has brought prosperity for generations of people, but also backbreaking toil for the rice farmers in its delta, who must spread the river's cargo of fertile mud evenly over their paddy fields. The nine branches into which the Mekong is divided at its estuary are linked by a network of thousands of channels and natural streams extending throughout the entire delta. In fact, the river has only eight natural branches, but because eight is considered an unlucky number, the inventive Vietnamese simply counted in one of the channels. Eight tributaries were transformed into nine and thus – hey presto! – the lucky number for a happy and contented life.

The tangle of rivers and streams irrigates an area of around 40,000 square kilometers (15,200 square miles); Vietnam's most fertile agricultural region is about as big as Switzerland, and is the only area where the precious rice crop can be harvested three times a year.

Travelers wishing to experience the unspoilt Mekong Delta should take the time to visit Vietnam's south, where they will have the opportunity to talk to the local people – always a fascinating experience in Vietnam. Open and honest, the people give insights into their day-to-day concerns and problems, which take on a strange familiarity when examined more closely. They enjoy discussing children, schools, and vocational training with foreign visitors. While they have learnt to cope with the hard life in the delta, they hope their children will have access to more opportunities in the future

1 Baguettes in Vietnam – none crisper. **2** Captain Bassac and his helmsman. **3** Young and old on a duck farm at Chau Doc. **4** Raising nets for the shipping.

1
2
3

than mere rice farming. Behind the folksy idyll of pointed hats, glittering rice paddies, and overflowing cornucopias of fruit is a pretty tough existence, initially concealed by the friendly, hospitable manner of the people. Smiling, they explain, "We regard happiness as an antidote to our hard work. When our backs are bent from working in the paddy fields, sighing and complaining only make life worse. But our inner life, our feelings and thoughts are far greater, and we can take pleasure in them regardless of our situation."

These proud, confident rice farmers still measure external prosperity and good fortune by the amount of rice they possess to feed their families and to trade on the markets. Even in the darkest times, they can always count on a little luck from the brilliant white rice grains.

And to make sure that nothing changes, they are careful to stay on the right side of their ancestors, fathers and forefathers, burying them in small temples in the middle of the fertile rice paddies as a good omen for the future – and an opportunity for them to communicate with their descendants. The men and women of the Mekong Delta often spend hours kneeling before their dead in the paddy fields, counting their incense sticks to ensure they have an odd number. One stick stands for the unity of the whole, three are effective in all kinds of problems, while seven belong to the wandering souls; the living seek strength by calling up answers from the past to questions concerning their own future.

Predicting just what the future will bring is difficult for these people in the delta, steeped in tradition. The older ones worry, "When the children move to the city, misery is on the way." But the children of the Mekong counter, "We don't want to grub around in the mud like our parents and grandparents." They longingly dream of life in nearby Ho Chi Minh City, where they would rather open a computer store or restaurant, or pursue other dreams purloined from their idols on the TV. Most, however, fail. And those that succeed are consumed by homesickness.

The river, the delta, this mysterious world of water has shaped the lives of these cheerful and easy-going people more than they know – or are willing to accept. And when they adopt new lifestyles outside the Mekong Delta, they soften the images of their new lives by adding a return ticket; on the waters of the Mekong, they allowed everything that could destroy their traditions and day-to-day lives to simply float away. This is their philosophy, an equilibrium that must not be lost.

"This must be paradise," say many visitors after exploring the

1 The nimble *Princess* and the serene rice barque. **2** Breakfast by the Mekong. **3** Hoist the flag, the *Bassac* is on its way. **4** A cozy berth on the Mekong. **5** and **6** Wedding by the wayside.

extensive network of rivers and channels and marveling at the rich harvests of fish, fruit, and vegetables. "This is paradise," comes the confident rejoinder from the South Vietnamese of the Mekong. Yet they also confirm that time in the delta cannot stand still. Some have already adjusted to the unfamiliar needs of a modern market economy and the ever-rising standards of hotels and restaurants. The smart business folk, vegetable farmers, and fish breeders want to discover how to deal with tourism, and how to unload their precious fish, fruit, and vegetables more rapidly onto the greedy markets in the exploding metropolis of Ho Chi Minh City, in as fresh a state as they are accustomed to.

A visit to the capital and university city of Can Tho is a worthwhile way to become familiar with this day-to-day life between water and woods, wilderness and city, and to understand it in more depth. Unfortunately, few roads lead to Can Tho and the journey is a long one. The busy A1 main road directly connects Saigon to the Mekong Delta. Plan at least five hours for the drive, although the journey is a mere 200 or so kilometers (120 miles). The adventure

1 Trial of courage on the Mekong – crossing a bamboo bridge. **2** Rice-paper factory for spring rolls. **3** The river is full – sampan rush hour on the Mekong. **4** The day the rains came – flooded main street of Can Tho.

of Mekong starts in Ho Chi Minh City. An early start is customary. And although we are traveling away from the city, we are trapped in an unbelievable throng of traffic which is known as the rush hour, but has absolutely nothing in common with our usual understanding of the phrase.

It is wise to cultivate the same equanimity as the Vietnamese themselves in order to understand why foreigners should avoid driving in Vietnam. Crossing Saigon is the first step on the Mekong adventure, and is an integral part of it. At a later stage of the expedition we can enjoy the beautiful countryside and marvel at the events taking place along the roadside. There's always something going on, in the best seats of this theater of life. It's well worth stopping to watch a wedding, or to buy a single cigarette from an old woman with a hawker's tray.

But if an aspiring Formula One champion is behind the wheel, things may become uncomfortable. Any willingness on his part to consider a gentler style of driving is short-lived. Fortunately, he is soon thwarted by our arrival at the ferry over the Hau, a tributary of the Mekong. Prepare for a long wait; this is the sole connection to Can Tho for vehicles.

Moored at the market hall directly on the banks of the Mekong is the Bassac, a wonderful wooden barque, offering cruises down the Mekong with accommodation. The ship has twelve cozy cabins, a fantastic sundeck, and a restaurant. Delicious Mekong specialties are served on the main deck. The Bassac moors on the riverbank overnight, and the Mekong dream begins.

The lifeline of the Mekong

What to see

Drive from Saigon to the Mekong Delta, taking in fascinating glimpses of daily life at the wayside. Arrive in the capital and university city of *Can Tho* at the jetty of the colonial-era old market hall.

Where to stay

In a cabin on the *Bassac*, a magnificently restored wooden rice barque from the Mekong Delta. The ship has twelve cozy cabins, a beautiful sundeck, and a restaurant.

Landlubbers will love the colonial-style *Victoria Hotel*:
Victoria Hotel, Cai Khe Ward, *Can Tho*.
Tel: 0084-71810111,
www.victoriahotels-asia.com

Where to eat and drink

The restaurant on the *Bassac* serves exquisite Mekong specialties and has an impressive wine list with an excellent selection of French wines.

4

Special recommendation

Take an excursion in the *Bassac's* dinghy to the small villages on the banks of the Mekong. Watch rice paper being produced, see where Vietnamese grapefruit grow, and how puffed rice is made.

Information

Transmekong, 97/10 Ngô Quyên, *Can Tho*.
Tel: 0084-913136024, e-mail: benoit@transmekong.com,
www.benoit.transmekong.com

Exotissimo Travel Vietnam Co Ltd, Saigon Finance Center
9 Dinh Tien Hoang, District 1, *Ho Chi Minh City.*
Tel: 0084-88251723-283,
e-mail: infoEXO@exotissimo.com,
go.vietnam@exotissimo.com,
www.exotissimo.com

1
2
NHA 1938 THO
PHAN-V-CUCNG
3
4

Breakfast with a Princess

Cruising Through the Labyrinth of the Nine Dragons

A tale of nine dragons, a comfortable rice barge, chirping cicadas, a beautiful princess, a mysterious villa, a fish with elephant's ears, a hotel director who knows his bird calls, and a floating market

Qiu Niu loves music, Ya Zi is fickle. Chao Feng thirsts after risk, Pu Lao's voice is a roar. San Mi plays with fire. Ba Xia drinks in sweet words – Fu Xi prefers literature. Bi An can distinguish good from evil, and Chi Wen is the toughest of all the nine dragons, devouring anything that crosses his path.

The Vietnamese in the delta are thoroughly familiar with the habits of their dragons; as dwellers in the low-lying regions, they suffer more from the nine beasts' fluctuating moods than all other Mekong dwellers from China to Cambodia. Chao Feng and Chi Wen, the two action fans among the dragons, are often bored and start fooling around, causing the Mekong to flood its banks. The dragons crow with malicious delight, and the farmers take the brunt of their sport. Vietnam's "rice bowl" overflows and the water washes the precious seedlings out of the soil; the harvest fails, and the backbreaking labor starts all over again. Nevertheless, the farmers maintain that "to live in peace with the dangerous Mekong, you need to place yourself at the mercy of the nine dragons." To do this, the Vietnamese perform a host of affectionate actions which can also be applied to everyday life. When conflict with the fabulous creatures is looming, flowers and incense sticks are classic choices for an initial peace offering. Even foreigners can easily grasp the mythology; the dragons have so many human traits that the stories mirror everyday life in both East and West – and that's just the way it should be.

The outlines of Can Tho, the provincial capital, emerge against the never-ending backdrop of rice paddies, and travelers on the long route from Saigon enter the Mekong's day-to-day routine. The first glimpse of the bustling life in the capital is enough to dispel any illusions about mysterious places concealed in tropical jungles; yet the charm of this vibrant city soon captivates new arrivals. With a population of 300,000, Can Tho is the largest city in the delta and the hub of all its waterways and roads. Its riverbank promenade, named after the valiant Hai Ba Trung sisters, is a lively scene. Attrac-

1 and **3** A juicy breakfast on the *Cai Be Princess*, Can Tho. **2** Former home of a fruit baron, Can Tho. **4** Victoria Hotel in Can Tho, colonial magnificence on the Mekong.

1 Cruising with a princess – *Cai Be Princess.* **2** Dawn breakfast on the *Cai Be Princess.* **3** and **4** Mekong fruit baroness. **5** Reception committee on the *Princess.* **6** Off we go, helmsman – maneuver along the Mekong.

tive garden cafés and restaurants with a magnificent view of the Mekong are set out on well-tended lawns shaded by palm trees at the confluence of Can Tho and Hau Giang. The restaurant owners go about attracting the attention of prospective customers in a civilized manner; there are no irritating hustlers to be seen, probably because beetle-browed "Uncle Ho" (Ho Chi Minh) is standing guard nearby. Gently smiling, the towering silver statue serves the lively South Vietnamese people as a silent reminder of the Communist government in Hanoi, which still has the ruling hand – even in the South.

The "People's Committee" in Can Tho takes a harder-hitting approach, playing quite a different tune in its daily refresher courses in party ideology. The loudspeakers burst into life at five in the morning, bellowing a propaganda song into the ears of the startled southerners. An unusual occurrence in the Vietnam of today, but one with a special history: after the liberation of Saigon, the headstrong, proud inhabitants of the Mekong delayed until the

4
5
6

very last minute before capitulating their city to their new rulers from the north.

At the end of the promenade stands a restored market hall from the French colonial era. The side of the hall which is open to the Mekong almost conceals the mooring berth for a ship of dark brown wood, the *Bassac*. For its French owner, Ben, the *Bassac* is the fulfillment of a lifelong dream. *Bassac* is the French name for Haut – or upper – River, along which his ship plies its route. Ben installed six double cabins with cozy berths and delightful bathrooms in the hull of the traditional rice barge, and sited a fashionable restaurant on the upper deck and a sun terrace on the steering deck.

The renovated ship has restored the spirit of the river to the Mekong Delta, hopes Ben, even though goods transport is increasingly in the hands of modern and, primarily, fast ships. Conversion of the *Bassac* took one year and was carried out in Chai Village, a shipbuilding community such as can be found only on the Mekong. Now its passengers can spin their own lifelong dreams on its upper deck, pondering the course of their lives. The bow of the *Bassac* nudges slowly but purposefully through the brown waters of the Mekong. The crew's friendly shout inviting us to a refreshing drink

on the captain's deck brings us back to reality – and what a pleasant place to be.

Many people find that Vietnam and its landscape inspire an indescribable, positive energy in them. Just add water, and their state of mind becomes positively mystical. The delicious specialties of the Mekong, simply and carefully prepared by the ship's cook, safeguard the fleshly aspect of our well-being. It's worth breaking the journey to Cai Be, a small town in the upper delta, to take short excursions in the dinghy of the *Bassac*; there is no shortage of fascinating sights. The banks are home to small family brickworks and clay pot factories, fruit and vegetable gardens, fish and shrimp farms. More contemplative travelers may prefer to remain on deck and enjoy the comfort of their lounger.

Occasional adventurers seeking to escape from civilization, however, will jump at the chance to forge their way through dense, steaming jungles, learning how to peel the grapefruit-like *pomelo* or make rice paper. Designated crew members attend willingly to guests' needs on land, too. In the evening, the rice barge with its luxury interior moors outside the little village of Tra On. The Mekong night draws in, clearly enfolding every living thing in its gray veil of twilight and intoxicating cascade. First the cicadas begin their tinny chirping, joined by cawing birds, quacking ducks, and croaking frogs. The performance begins with a cheerful greeting and rises to a surging crescendo before the last rays of the sun escape over the horizon. The Mekong night begins – and ends abruptly in terrifying silence. A silence that becomes so unnerving that there is no possibility of turning over and going back to sleep in the snug berth. But soon the sun resumes control of the world. The day begins, the *Bassac* hoists anchor, plunging full speed ahead into the hubbub of the broad waterways, where any final dreams of remote bays and dancing butterflies are scattered. Here, life leaps from the spume flung up by the freighters, speedboats, and dinghies. Melons, kohlrabi, cucumbers, tomatoes, and onions, more and more boatloads of onions overtake the leisurely *Bassac*, all hurrying to reach the floating market of Cai Be. The old rice barge pants to keep up with the crowd; the *Princess* awaits, and the familiar rule "Never keep a lady waiting" also applies in Vietnam.

By the time the *Cai Be Princess* finally draws up alongside and affectionately nudges the old timbers of the *Bassac*, everyone loves her. This beautiful sampan is a house-boat in black ebony picked out in gold. Elegant, slim, and maneuverable, she has a touch of colonial decadence which goes unnoticed in the overall beauty of its appearance; the soft, comfortable loungers into which passengers sink blissfully receive more attention. The sampan is the ideal

1 to **3** Le Longainier, gourmet restaurant in the Mekong Delta. **4** Elephant ear fish, delicacy from the depths of the river. **5** and **6** *Lau*, the national specialty: a hotpot of broth with fish, seafood, and vegetables, simmering on the table.

method of transport for gliding through the little market of Cai Be and down narrow side channels, past fishing nets, and under low-hanging chains of bamboo. Once, the prosperous fruit-and-vegetable barons lived in villas hidden in the jungle and accessible only via private routes. One such villa is now a superb restaurant named Le Longanier de Phu An, accessible only with the *Princess*. Surrounded by pomelo, longan, mango, coconut, and banana trees, the restaurant is furnished with antiques from the 1930s. So much imposing luxury in the heart of the Mekong Delta may be surprising, but when we discover that the land of the delta itself was reclaimed only at enormous effort in the mid-19th century under the direction of the French "colons," it is easy to understand that the French brought some of their lifestyle with them to their new jungle home.

Guests are welcomed in the tropical garden of the two-storey villa by an elegant, *ao dai*-clad Vietnamese lady. A tour of the villa convinces us that this is the life. Under the slowly rotating ceiling fan of the terrace, a cool drink in hand, we muse over the last secret of the day – the fish with elephant ears.

The elephant ear fish is considered to be the delta's most exquisite specialty. It is served whole, upright in a bamboo frame. Take a piece of rice paper, cover it with rice, vegetables, and crisp chunks of fish, roll it up and eat it, dipping the whole in wonderful sauces. At least, so the menu says. Not a simple procedure, but help is at

1 and **3** Tropical atmosphere and colonial charm: Victoria-Hotel in Can Tho. **2** Deluxe rooms with a view of the river. **4** German director Hanno Stamm and his top team.

hand. Just glance over to where the quiet giggles are coming from, and an elegant "princess" is quickly on hand to assist, turning her guests into genuine kings and queens.

But the crew of the *Cai Be Princess* eventually call on us to take our leave. The delta is extensive, and the trip to Vinh Long is upstream. The peacefully rocking timbers of the sampan are exchanged for the rattling metal of a Toyota Landcruiser and we return to Can Tho by road, exchanging berths and cabins for comfort and air-conditioning. The Victoria Hotel in Can Tho, at the heart of the Mekong Delta, offers everything we hadn't realized we were missing. Its comfortable atmosphere wins us over, and we explore the beautiful corners of the hotel park, eagerly heeding the calls of the brightly colored birds. German hotel director Hanno Stamm is happy to point out the individual species. Hanno and his English partner Richard Craik are internationally recognized ornithologists specializing in the 850-plus species in Vietnam.

3

They are thoroughly familiar with the 15 bird reserves in Vietnam, and organize excursions to the reserves under Richard's leadership. It's a novel idea which has proved popular, and is a fine way of making in-depth contact with Vietnam's breathtaking natural world.

Next morning, just before six when the sun is making its first attempt to add sparkle to the brown waters of the Mekong, a further excursion is planned: a visit to the floating market of Cai Rang – the best opportunity to experience traditional day-to-day life along the Mekong.

Everything follows the rules arranged on the water, from boat to boat, from sailor to sailor – all under the watchful gaze of the good spirits. There isn't a ship, sampan, or dinghy on the river without the demonic gaze of the red and white eyes painted on its bow. These eyes are the only power that can quell the mighty waters of the Mekong. Without the eyes, not a single kohlrabi or pineapple would reach the market, not a single child would arrive at school, and not a single tourist would visit the loveliest market on the Mekong Delta.

In the labyrinth of the nine dragons

What to see
The floating markets of Cai Be and Cai Rang. Brick and clay pot manufacture in the environs of Can Tho.
The riverbank promenade with its attractive garden cafés and enormous statue of Ho Chi Minh, avenue of palms and small historic quarter on the banks of the Mekong.

Where to stay
Bassac, Transmekong, 97/10 Ngo Quyen, *Can Tho*.
Tel: 0084-913136024, e-mail: benoit@transmekong.com, http://benoit.transmekong.com.
Victoria Hotel, Cai Khe Ward, *Can Tho*. Tel: 0084-71810111, www.victoriahotels-asia.com

Where to eat and drink
Restaurant Le Longanier, Mekong Horizon.
Tel: 0084-73924658, e-mail: mekonghorizon@yahoo.com
Can Tho Market Hall, Mekong fish specialties,
e-mail: benoit@transmekong.com

4

Special recommendations
Boat rides in the traditional sampans along the narrow channels and tributaries of the Mekong. Bird-watching with specialists Richard Craik and Hanno Stamm, from early morning to twilight. Vietnam has around 850 species of birds, including 5 which are found only in South Vietnam.
e-mail: richard@vietnambirding.com,
www.vietnambirding.com

Information
Cai Be Princess, Mekong Horizon, Head Office, 49 Hamlet 5, *Phu An*. Tel: 0084-73924658,
e-mail: mekonghorizon@yahoo.com

Exotissimo Travel Vietnam Co Ltd, Saigon Finance Center
9 Dinh Tien Hoang, District 1, *Ho-Chi-Minh-City.*
Tel: 0084-88251723-283
e-mail: infoEXO@exotissimo.com,
go.vietnam@exotissimo.com,
www.exotissimo.com

Fish Farm in the Living Room

The Floating Houses of Chau Doc

A holy mountain, diving birds, a market paradise, a mysterious man, a shrouded figure, an ocean of flowers, and a reserve for mosquitoes, birds, and prostrate observers.

The holy mountain calls – and many answer. In the mornings around five o'clock, before cockcrow and before the sun has even opened its eyes, the narrow road to the summit is already black with people. Those who elect to drive to the top will save themselves aching muscles, but probably earn a guilty conscience at the sight of the energetic Vietnamese, many of whom start their day with tai chi exercises while others use the early hour to pray. The holy mountain of Nui Sam, just outside the village of Chau Doc, welcomes them all.

The summit, which is not a peak but actually a broad plateau 230 meters (755 feet) above sea level, unfolds a panoramic view of the flat, expansive landscape which is unequalled in the whole of the Mekong Delta. From up here, the water in the rice paddies glitters like diamonds in the first rays of the sun. The comparison is deliberate; they are the true treasures of nature, sending signals of light to humanity as a reminder of their vulnerability. And humanity seems to understand. The people wait silently in these minutes between night and day. Even the rooster is silent, and no cameras are heard. Then the light, early mist rises to the clouds, the sun caresses the morning gymnasts, and the rooster takes a deep breath, finally able to throw out his breast with pride and trumpet his cock-a-doodle-doo into the new morning. The horizon slashes a sharp boundary between earth and sky as if it had something to hide. And perhaps it does. Beyond the horizon the landscape rolls onward, deep into Vietnam's history. To the northwest is Vietnam's neighbor Cambodia. While the Vietnamese can now turn their eyes to that direction once more, they are unwilling to look back. For years, the neighboring country represented the source of the calamity that was the Khmer Rouge. Pol Pot's guards repeatedly terrorized the farmers in the border regions. In 1978, the Vietnamese finally succeeded in defending themselves, and since then there has been peace.

To the southwest lies the Gulf of Thailand, where the island of Phu Quoc, although 120 kilometers (72 miles) away, is occasionally

1 A grave in the rice fields, Chau Doc. **2** Mekong-style. **3** The holy mountain of Nui Sam: "Cambodia is over there." **4** View from Victoria Hotel, Chau Doc; Phnom Penh is straight ahead, Ha Tien to the left.

1 and **3** A family affair: floating fish farm at Chau Doc. **2** The bird reserve at Tra Su. **4** and **5** Before and after: pangasius, a tasty delicacy. **6** Rice farmer under sugar palms near Chau Doc.

visible according to its proud Vietnamese owners. "The island once belonged to Cambodia," explains a friendly morning gymnast, "but that was a long time ago, and nobody's going to rehash old arguments."

In the southeast we can sense Can Tho, our last stop. A road leads directly from the foot of Nui Sam towards Chau Doc in the northeast, running straight for five kilometers (3 miles). The view from the mountain with its magnificent panorama gives us our first impression of the sheer size of the region through which we are traveling. And our ideas concerning the interplay of water and land adopt a new, clearer dimension.

In comparison, the road back to Chau Doc is the smallest unit of measurement. On its lower stretches we can indulge in a good deed in front of the Tay An Pagoda; by paying a couple of dong to release a "lucky bird" from its bamboo cage and making a wish as it flies away. Far from being lucky, however, these poor creatures are often so exhausted from their imprisonment that their ransom is paid too late. Distractedly flapping, they plunge into a nose-dive and make an uncontrolled crash landing to end in sparrow nirvana. A few kilometers further, we encounter more attractive imagery. The little market in Chau Doc is positively bursting at the seams with color: flowers, fruit, and fish as far as the eye can see. Friendly market women patiently explain the names of the treasures they

carry from the Mekong Delta. The market has such a rich variety of produce on offer that we are gripped by an irresistible idea: this must have been paradise, the Garden of Eden, which is always described in this way. Our idea takes on reality in the bustle of the market.

The riverbank promenade is opposite the market. Newly renovated with some pretty gross neon candelabra, it is a meeting point for young and old. Inquisitive foreigners are not a problem; quite the opposite, in fact – a cheery exchange of "Hello" spreads good humor all round. This is the departure point for private boats going to all corners of the upper Mekong. Tagging along on a short trip is enjoyable, provided you don't mind sitting on fishnets coated with fresh scales. However, speedboat trips to Cambodia are better booked in the Victoria Hotel. The hotel is at the end of the promenade; part of its terrace, the River View Room, is practically in the river itself. Breakfast here is a memorable experience. Over fresh orange juice, rich croissants, and crisp baguette said by the French to be better than the originals in France, our view straight ahead extends to Cambodia, while to the left we see the fishing boats of Can Tho and to the right the famous floating houses – an enormous suburb bobbing on rafts of empty metal barrels in the Mekong.

Families here have farmed the delicious pangasius fish for generations – directly in the living rooms of their houseboats. These angular, rocking pontoons are the focal points of whole lives and careers. The main room houses the stove and dining area and has a

large hole in its floor sealed with nets which extend into the river itself. The waters flow through the nets, catching the precious fish, which can be kept under permanent observation from above and fed with rice flour or bananas. A narrow. plank walkway leads from this central room to the other houses of the fish farm, all linked together by thick hawsers. The family with its three children thus retains full control over its specialty, the valuable pangasius, a type of catfish principally found in the Mekong. At eight months the fishes weigh a good two kilograms and are ready for their last long journey. Pangasius is a delicacy much sought after not only by the Saigonese and luxury restaurants; it is now popular all over the world and has taken over as Vietnam's top export.

After this final expedition into the ever rocking world of water, we are eager to feel firm ground under our feet again, somewhere along the banks of the Mekong. Bewildered by the enormous choice of attractive excursions, we helplessly consider our options, until Mr. Man has an idea. The elegantly dressed Vietnamese with the severe gaze is the general manager in the Victoria Hotel team, a man of many secrets and endless fascination. He launches into flawless French, switches to American English to chat to guests, and then laughs heartily at a joke in his mother tongue. During his career he has held "executive positions" with the Americans, and also headed Air France in Saigon. He is an almost unrivaled expert on the mercurial nature of life in Vietnam. Now he concentrates on pampering the guests in his hotel and supervising his young team with affectionate, fatherly authority. "They are all children of the Mekong," he explains, his voice taking on a new warmth, "and they are the future of the Mekong. I do all I can to give them a training."

We believe him. Perhaps tourism will bring prosperity to everyone. In any case, his views are well received and so are the suggestions he makes for the excursion: Sa Dec flower village, Tra Su bird reserve.

A "child of the Mekong" pulls up in front of the hotel at eight on the dot, driving an old US military jeep. 21-year-old Tri is familiar with the route to Sa Dec and the bird reserve. And he also knows exactly how to get to where he wants to go in life. His goal is independence, being the master of his own decisions for himself and, in the future, for a family: from tourist guide to millionaire. The American dream in the Mekong Delta. And Tri has already begun to live his dream. Some time ago he bought an original US military jeep from the Victoria Hotel and painstakingly restored the ancient junk-heap. Now he drives tourists through his home country, the Mekong Delta, as an independent guide, while repaying the loan to the hotel. Doesn't he have a problem with the idea of driving

1 Tran Cam Tu and the team of Victoria Hotel, Chau Doc. **2** Slender Monkey Bridge. **3** Visiting mom – pharmacist Mrs. Ngoc. **4** A Mekong beauty. **5** Who's there? – it's the charming receptionist.

around in "war equipment" which may have been used to cause much suffering? "Well, heck," he beams, "the war's over, you know – we want to live in the future, not the past." He guns the engine of his US jeep and tells us, "Tourists sometimes ask me, Hey, Mr. Tri, which way to the war?"

A second "child of the Mekong" is napping in the back of the jeep. The slight, swathed form had politely asked whether she could join the ride to Sa Dec, the village of flowers. It is her home; she wants to visit her mother. No problem; but as the kilometers and miles unfold, so does our curiosity about the sleeping passenger, who bounces closer to us with every pothole. Who's in there? Her name is Lam, she is 20 years old. When she removes her face mask

Could this be paradise?

The market at Chau Doc is no more crowded than other markets in Vietnam, but it's crammed with so much delicious fruit, vegetables, and fish that there's hardly room to move. Yet the market women are a little friendlier to visitors here than elsewhere – perhaps because they're so proud of their appetizing, fragrant, and tasty wares. They are happy to let us sample the produce, and some even attempt, in a cascade of incomprehensible yet mellifluous words and graphic gestures, to explain how the various plants grow.

Prices, however, should not be mentioned. The people here would never understand the exorbitant amounts Westerners pay for a mango in a delicatessen store.

In paradise: fruit, snakes, and fish at the colorful market of Chau Doc.

1 The pool in the Mekong – the terrace of Victoria Hotel, Chau Doc. **2** Guaranteed fresh: fish from the Mekong. **3** As elegant as a cruise liner – Victoria Hotel, the pearl of the Mekong. **4** On the banks of the Mekong – breakfast at sunrise. **5** Main gate of Rach Gia, a vibrant town on the Gulf of Thailand.

and sunglasses we see who she is. Lam is the receptionist from the Victoria Hotel. Thanks to her excellent English, she is in charge of welcoming the new international arrivals. Lam cordially quizzes them about customs and habits in their countries, and they take delight in her interest; in this way, she has amassed a great deal of knowledge about the people who come and go in her hotel. She plans to go to America, to study and learn languages. Her mother is afraid that Lam will lose the connection to her home. Wouldn't it be better for her to take over her mother's pharmacy, start a family with a nice man, and rear her children on the Mekong? Lam smiles, certain that she will return – after experiencing life in other countries for herself.

And having seen her home village of Sa Dec, we are certain, too. The glorious village is a sea of color. Even non-gardening enthusiasts are in ecstasy. We'd love to gather armfuls of bouquets, fill the whole jeep with flowerpots. Tri is concerned about the heat, Lam coolly reminds us of the lovely bouquets available in the hotel, and her mother laughs and invites us in to eat.

Mangroves to the left, swamps to the right, and flocks of birds in the middle. Here, amid the musty smell of mold and surrounded by mosquitoes eager to attack the white-skinned targets, we lie motionless for hours in the boats, silent but happy, watching the birds flitting around. The most zealous bird-watching sleuths commission the professional guidance of ornithologists such as Hanno Stamm or Richard Craik, rowing through Tra-Su National Park in little aluminum canoes. Equipped with binoculars, camera, and notebook, we rapidly learn how to pick out the birds among the dense mangroves and determine their species, under the approving eye of the ornithologists.

They also readily supply information on other secrets of this vulnerable natural world. No one is more keenly aware than they are of the threat looming over these final outposts of a tropical primeval landscape.

Mekong Delta and Chau Doc

What to see
Early morning walk to the holy mountain of *Nui Sam*, with view of Cambodia. The *Tay An Pagoda* and the "luck birds," the paradise of *Chau Doc* market, and riverside promenade.

Where to stay
Victoria Hotel Chau Doc, 32 Le Loi St.
Tel: 0084-76865010, fax: 0084-76865020,
e-mail: gm.cantho@victoriahotels-asia.com,
www.victoriahotels-asia.com

What to eat and drink
The best street vendors are around the market on *Le Cong Than* Street, where all the delicacies of the Mekong are cooked up. A treat for inquisitive gourmets.
Bassac Restaurant in *Victoria Hotel* serves imaginative cuisine that is a fusion of Western and Asian influences.

Special recommendations
The floating houses of *Chau Doc* and their in-house fish farms.
The village of flowers *Sa Dec* and the *Tra Su* bird reserve.
The terrace of *Victoria Hotel*, Chau Doc with *River View Room*, suspended over the Mekong.
Speedboat excursion from the jetty of the *Victoria Hotel*, Chau Doc to Phnom Penh, Cambodia. The four-hour trip takes place daily.

Information
Speedboot Cambodia, *Victoria Hotel Chau Doc*,
32 Le Loi St. Tel: 0084-76865010, fax: 0084-76865020,
e-mail: gm.cantho@victoriahotels-asia.com,
www.victoriahotels-asia.com

Exotissimo Travel Vietnam Co Ltd, Saigon Finance Center,
9 Dinh Tien Hoang, District 1, *Ho-Chi-Minh-City*
Tel 0084-88251723-283
e-mail: infoEXO@exotissimo.com,
go.vietnam@exotissimo.com,
www.exotissimo.com

1

2

3

4

Relaxing on White Beaches

Phu Quoc – Island Paradise on the Gulf of Thailand

Saigon, markets, Mekong, Mass.
Overwhelmed by the wealth of impressions from Ho Chi Minh City?
Take time out on Phu Quoc – sun, sand, and inner peace.

Has the pilot of this incredible, sonorously droning prop plane taken a wrong turning? Is it a mirage, or is there really a lonely island in the crystalline waters, just visible under the right wing? A glance out of the cabin window almost hurts the eyes, so bright is the contrast between the white sand of the beach and the blue sky. But it's true. This is Phu Quoc – shades of the Caribbean.
A relaxed atmosphere already reigns in the tiny airport. No cries of "Hey, mister!" from itinerant vendors. Friendly islanders offer their hotels and guesthouses with some restraint. The pleasant breeze eases cool sea air between skin and clothes. At last, the chance to recover for a few days from the perpetually sticky shirts and humid air of the delta.
On the western side of the island, at Cassia Cottage on the white beach of Ba Keo, we are awaited by the "cinnamon king of Yen Bai." The respectful title was given to American Mark Barnett by his friends. Mark has been a spice trader in Vietnam for 16 years, harvesting pepper on Phu Quoc; however, his speciality is farming cassia, or cinnamon, in the district of Yen Bai in the remote and inaccessible high north. His cozy bungalow resort on Phu Quoc is named Cassia Cottage. Whenever time allows, he joins his Vietnamese team and cares for his guests himself. Mark's sundowners are heavenly, and the distance from bungalow to sea is all of a 50-meter (160 feet) stroll between the coconut palms and the swimming pool. There, glass in hand, his guests await the sunset. It's a regular evening ritual which not even the veteran islanders can shake off; this is the very best place in Vietnam to experience sunset on the beach. This has something to do not only with the relaxed "Bacardi feeling," but also quite simply the fact that the beaches face exactly west, while all the mainland beaches face east. Romantics on the mainland are therefore advised to watch the sunrise instead. A new day begins, adventure is in the air. Islands are there to be explored. But how? Do we dare to mount a scooter without Xe Om? It's worth a try. Xe Om means "embrace" – in this case, the passenger embracing the scooter driver. And of course, the driver

1 Lucky Man, the fisher of Phu Quoc. **2** Family bathtime under the waterfall at the center of the island. **3** Lunchtime buffet on the palm-fringed beach. **4** Coconut palms and coral reefs on "Pepper Island".

1 Hotel beach, Cassia Cottage. 2 Tropical gardens and palm village by the ocean. 3 Cassia Cottage: room with a view over the pool and the ocean. 4 Small fish in the net at Phu Quoc beach. 5 Big fish at the fish farm at Ganh Dau, in the island's north.

needs to be paid. So let's try going it alone! The roads are good, the mopeds have automatic gears, and it's a lot of fun. One word of warning, though: never use the front brake, not even in an emergency! It's so easy to jam the brake when panic sets in – an unpleasant occurrence that can happen to the most seasoned riders. To avoid the problem, try the simple trick of wrapping a scarf or handkerchief around the brake lever. This will make you stop and think and prevent you from braking automatically. The Vietnamese are naturally aware of the problem, but employ a simple solution: they simply deactivate the front brake.

"Go south, easy rider" – wherever you start your ride, going south is a good idea. The reddish sand track leads past glorious empty beaches, ending in the picturesque fishing village of An Thoi. It's well worth a longer stay; the An Thoi Islands off the coast are among Vietnam's most beautiful diving and snorkeling locations.

From the northern tip of the island, the name of which, incidentally, means "beautiful country," we can look across the rolling hills as far as Cambodia in clear weather. The island's national park is also located here. When returning to the west coast, it's worth visiting the "land of pepper" around Khu Tuong. The pepper plantations are easy to spot: the green plants growing up their long stakes are up to three meters (10 feet) high. The plantation owners are friendly and can recount many an exciting and informative tale about their crop.

Ladies and gentlemen, please start your engines. Anyone who has managed to avoid problems with the front brake thus far will look forward to the last stage of our scooter expedition on this island of good humor. We're heading west again, to the idyllic beaches – the call of the sunset – past small fishing villages and the pretty capital of Duong Dong.

No need for map or compass to find the town. Napoleon claimed that he could recognize his home island of Corsica blindfolded from the scent of its herbs, and the same applies to the capital of Phu Quoc. But if you'll pardon me for saying so, what characterizes Duong Dong isn't the scent of herbs – it's the smell of fish. Many might consider it the finest fragrance in the world, because the source of the smell is also a source of prosperity and rich flavor: Nuoc Mam, Vietnam's delicious fish sauce. A complex fermentation

1 Robinson Crusoe had it harder – lunch on the beach with perfect service. **2** Brand-new, but in the old colonial style – La Veranda set out for a candlelit dinner. **3** Only found on Phu Quoc – sunset over the ocean. **4** Cocktail bar at La Veranda.

process is employed to coax great vats of dried sardines into maturing to produce the tasty brew. Vietnam supplies the whole world; the sauce is one of the country's top exports.

And the funniest sign in Vietnam is at the security check of the airport check-in desks. It's the sign warning passengers that Nuoc Mam is not permitted in their hold baggage – and it's posted next to the sign prohibiting weapons.

Another sign on the return journey is also surprising. It depicts larger-than-life dogs which some may recognize as Rhodesian Ridgebacks. They are bred on the island as distant cousins of the Phu Quoc dog, naturally complete with their typical ridge of fur down the spine. The large breeding kennels are worth a visit. The breeder is a smart, young Vietnamese who also supplies interesting information on the history of the island and sells pearls from the crystal-clear seas, produced by the pearl oyster farms on the west coast.

This coast so full of precious things occasionally brings particularly good fortune. "Lucky Man One" is a recipient of its bounty. We notice him at the filling station, transporting an extra wide load on his Honda. The lateral fins of a giant ray hang down, its central eye staring in disgust at its audience, and the dangerous whip-like sting carefully lashed to the scooter. 49-year-old fisherman Nguyen Van Hoang moves carefully to avoid damaging his passenger, which he plans to sell at the market for around 720,000 dong.

"Lucky Man Two" almost causes a pile-up, but fortunately our trick of the scarf on the front brake lever saves the day and our scooter glides slowly to a halt. The 36-year-old fisherman Hau Duc Hoang is a sight for the gods. He is struggling along, clasping his good fortune, a 20-kilogram (44 pound) tunafish for which the buyer in Doung Dong will offer him around 20 US dollars. But before he

2

3

can celebrate, he must walk another four kilometers (2.4 miles) with his cargo.

Fortunately, all we have to do is step on the gas of our now dust-encrusted moped. And yet we're left wondering – are all lucky fishermen called Hoang?

Along the beach, a mere 400 meters (1,300 feet) from Cassia Cottage, a different world begins. La Veranda is the island's most modern resort, with a captivating air of luxury in its bungalows tastefully grouped around the big tropical garden.

The beach is neatly tended, and the resort is designed for enjoying the sunset from comfortable basket chairs with a champagne bucket nearby – a Caribbean vision that almost makes us forget where we actually are – which also inspires the temptation to peek into the future. Of course, we hope that all the small dreams, the modest expectations, and hopes in such major projects will not end up buried and invisible in the white sands.

Harry Belafonte's wonderful song, "Oh, island in the sun ..." the classic soundtrack for island dreams, plays loud and clear in our minds on the 400 meters (1,300 feet) of road back to Cassias Cottage: "... her shores will always be home to me."

Phu Quoc – the island paradise

What to see

The diving and snorkeling paradise of the *An Thoi Islands* is among Vietnam's most beautiful underwater locations, and is also a breathtaking experience for non-divers. The traditional fishing village of *An Thoi* is nearby.

The pepper plantations at *Khu Tuong* in the southwest, the capital of Duong Dong with its quaint lanes and a fish-sauce factory are worth visiting.

The *Phu Quoc dogs*, at the well-run breeding farm owned by a Vietnamese specialist, will make animal lovers' hearts beat faster.

Where to stay

Cassia Cottage, Khu Pho 1, Duong Dong Beach, *Phu Quoc Island*. Tel: 0084-77848395, fax: 0084-49284967, e-mail: cassiacottage@cassiacottage.com, www.cassiacottage.com.

La Veranda, Duong Dong Beach, Tran Hung Dao St., *Phu Quoc Island*. Tel: 0084-877982988, fax: 0084-877982998, e-mail: contact@laverandaresort.com, www.laverandaresort.com

4

Where to eat and drink

The little fishing port of *Duong Dong* has a host of lively bars where the locals spend their evenings. Foreigners are welcome, but are charged higher prices than the islanders. Fans of beach vacations will love the palm-shaded restaurants at *Cassia Cottage* and the exclusive veranda at *La Veranda*.

Special recommendation

A tour of the island on your own fully automatic scooter is a lot of fun and quick to learn. It's easy to organize your own excursion on a fishing boat: ask the fishermen personally in *Duong Dong* harbor. The sunset is the highlight of the evening; *Phu Quoc*, with its west-facing beaches, offers the finest sunset views in Vietnam.

Information

Exotissimo Travel Vietnam Co Ltd, Saigon Finance Center
9 Dinh Tien Hoang, District 1, *Ho-Chi-Minh-City*
Tel: 0084-88251723-283,
e-mail: infoEXO@exotissimo.com,
go.vietnam@exotissimo.com,
www.exotissimo.com

Rubber, coffee, manioc, and pepper – the riches of the highlands.

From the Jungle to the Mountains

The Highlands of the South

Living in the Lap of Luxury, French-style

Dalat and the Southern Highlands

Dalat is the perfect example of Vietnamese wisdom: the art of retaining the best from their colonial past and adapting it to suit their own culture. All there is to see, hear, and taste in Dalat contains constant memories of the French colonial era, giving the city a unique flair.

Traveling from the Mekong into the mountains is more than a trip from sea level to the mountains. It is a journey between worlds, and into the past: into an era which has shaped modern-day Vietnam more powerfully than any other. At the zenith of the colonial era, with its economic boom, the sky was the limit for Vietnamese and French alike. At a location 1,475 meters (4,800 feet) above sea level, surrounded by forests, coffee plantations, and vegetable gardens, they began in 1912 to build up their "city of eternal spring" from nothing: Dalat. In the mid-1920s, Dalat was the most popular city in Vietnam. Even in the summer months, when Saigon's French population drooped exhausted and homesick in the heat, the temperature in Dalat was a temperate 15 to 24° C.

The climate is still unchanged – and the city is experiencing a rebirth, this time with the bittersweet charm of nostalgia. The elegant villas once inhabited by the French now house prosperous businesspeople of all nations or have been converted into elegant little hotels. Dalat is the perfect place to live in the lap of luxury, French-style – better than anywhere else in Vietnam. Perhaps it is also the least typical Vietnamese city in the country. To explain the city, we hand over to guest author Antoine Sirot, General Manager of the legendary Dalat Palace Hotel. A Frenchman in Dalat who drives his guests through his favorite city in an ancient Citroën, exuding wit and charm, smoking a *Gauloise noire*, gesticulating wildly, and turning round to chat to his guests while still steering. The perfect chauffeur! Here's his report:

"All there is to see: Dalat is a unique city, planned to the last detail on the drawing board by the best town planners and architects of the early 20th century. Names such as Hebrard, Lagisquet, and Mounet supported the idea of building a modern city for a new generation of people, fusing Eastern and Western influences and thus surpassing all existing cultures.

1 The home of the last emperor – now the guests here live like kings: Dalat Palace. **2** Honeymoon in the Valley of Love, the dream of all Vietnamese. **3** Putting green at Dalat – a golfer's dream. **4** Petit déjeuner with magnificent view – the breakfast terrace of the Dalat Palace.

1 The Presidential Suite – not only for presidents. **2** The keys to paradise – Sofitel Dalat Palace. **3** Such green as dreams are made on: Dalat Palace Golf Club. **4** A breakfast buffet fit for a king. **5** New recipes in an old villa.

When we look at the city today, in all its nostalgia, we sense that those planners actually attained their goal in the first five decades of the century. All its buildings were designed in contemporary modern style, paying constant and sensitive attention to the overall aesthetic impression. The result is stunning: a French suburban style with widely separated villas, gardens, lakes, and a golf course in the center. The French adopted it as a piece of home in Southeast Asia, in the country then called Indochina.

All there is to hear: The planners also allowed for the 'good' French habit of spending hours of the day in cafés. Today, Dalat's inhabitants are still enjoying the results! A new slant is that old French melodies are played on the café terraces. Many songs of the past are again back in currency, but in their own Vietnamese versions. Even French songs from the 1980s are still being sung, long after the French have left Vietnam. Sometimes I go to a dance hall and sing 'Comme Toi' as a duet with a young Vietnamese singer – I sing in French, he sings in Vietnamese.

All there is to smell: We drink in the intoxicating scent of geraniums, hydrangeas, and roses, which is reminiscent of the villages of France as it mingles with the fragrance of coffee. However, the latter component is a relatively recent arrival, and was sorely missed in the beginning. Vietnam is originally a tea-drinking country by tradition, and did not adopt coffee as a social beverage until much later. Coffee began to be drunk in small groups in cafés, but the

French 'café filtre' did not find its way over here for a long time. Anyone who has already ordered this coffee in Vietnam is aware of the significance of the coffee's long journey, drop by drop, from filter to cup. The captivating scent of coffee is part of day-to-day life in Dalat, not only on the café terraces. Many stores in the center sell freshly roasted beans of the superb local highland coffee.

All there is to taste: I was impressed the most by my first visit to Dalat Market. An incredible array of vegetables – I even found huge globe artichokes. I did some research on the origins of this magnificent and delicious produce, and came across an interesting story. It begins on the farm of Monsieur Borel in 1920. The farm still exists today, and the bounteous harvests are still produced by the estates of the past. An old Frenchman was ecstatic at the taste of an artichoke from there, and said, 'I haven't had an artichoke as tasty as these for 50 years. They remind me of vegetables from my youth.'

A famous French dish from Dalat is still served in many restaurants today. Its name is *lagu*, which translates as 'ragout' – the Vietnamese cannot roll their 'r's. *Lagu* comprises the traditional hearty meat stew with vegetables, or 'ragout,' which is a famous winter dish in French provincial cooking. It has become a hit, even in modern Vietnamese cuisine. Both French and Vietnamese eat the stew with enthusiasm, mopping up the gravy with chunks of baguette. There is naturally a small cultural difference: instead of Dijon mustard, the Vietnamese prefer a more powerful concoction of chili sauce.

These are just a few aspects of Dalat, my home town for the past five years, which I would like to highlight; the Vietnamese are skilful at distinguishing good things from bad. The really bad things are

1 Train to nowhere – the closed railway station at Dalat. **2** "Professor Vegetable" and his organic babies. **3** Traditional vegetable farming – the French brought vegetables to Dalat. **4** Crazy House – experimental architecture by Vietnamese artist Hang Nga. **5** A delighted golfing couple from Austria.

simply thrown away and forgotten as quickly as possible. Smart people."

Drawing breath between the interesting discourse and the next *noire*, Monsieur Antoine crashes the ancient Citroën into first gear. Dalat has plenty to offer, such as the golf course on the lake – the best-kept greens in Vietnam, according to connoisseurs, and certainly the first. The course was built by the last Emperor of Vietnam, His Excellency Bao Dai. Blessed with the twin gifts of good taste and plenty of time, he spent the summer in an enchanting Art Deco villa in Dalat. Even non-golfers are astonished when they see the 18-hole course.

The astonishment continues when visitors encounter the Valley of Love. A short distance from Xuan Huong Lake, it is an absolute must for bridal couples from all over the country. This is where weddings take place. In an atmosphere reminiscent of Disneyland,

the newlyweds paddle plastic swans over the artificial lake as photos are taken for their wedding album. It seems to generate happiness; the place is full of giggling brides tossing their long veils coquettishly against the sun. The grooms are more composed, struggling to maintain a solemn expression.

Over the next hill a few kilometers away, "Professor Vegetable" has other problems. Dr. Nguyen Ba Hung, a highly reputable yet humorous scientist with the air of a Gyro Gearloose, that appealing, eccentric inventor, is concerned about his organically grown baby vegetables. His carrots, spring onions, green beans, and fennel have an outstanding organic purity which is found nowhere else. Dr. Hung's strictly organic farming principles are based on the traditions of French farmers, but he is now being forced to move in new directions. Soon, the fertile fields around Dalat will no longer deliver their accustomed quality – decades of fertilizer have depleted the earth. To maintain the quality of the famous vegetables, he is forced to employ organic farming methods. Dr. Hung is on the best road to success. His delicious mini-vegetables, by the way, can already be found in the breakfast buffets of the best hotels.

Dalat – living in the lap of luxury, French-style

What to see

Dalat's now disused railway station with steam locomotives and cars from the colonial era, with rails leading nowhere. The elegant villa district with its bittersweet witnesses to better times. The Art Deco villa of the last Emperor, Bao Dai. The coffee plantations, organic vegetable farm of "Professor Vegetable," and colorful fields of flowers. Crazy House: experimental architecture by an idiosyncratic Vietnamese artist. The Valley of Love at Xuan Huong Lake, a meeting point for newlyweds and couples. The stylish Dalat Palace Golf Club, extending between the hotel and the lake, is Vietnam's most beautiful golf course.

Where to stay

Sofitel Dalat Palace Hotel, 12 Tran Phu St., *Dalat*.
Tel: 0084-863825444, fax: 0084-863825666,
e-mail: sofitel@vnn.vn, www.sofitel.com.

Novotel Dalat, 7 Tran Phu St., *Dalat*. Tel: 0084-63825777,
fax: 0084-63825888, e-mail: novotel@vnn.vn,
www.novotel-asia.com

5

Where to eat and drink

Fine French coffee can be had at *Café de la Poste*, between the old post office and the *Novotel*.
Café Tung, 6 Khu Hoa Binh, is still firmly rooted in the past; Jacques Brel's chansons still sigh from the record player.
A candlelit dinner in the restaurant of the *Dalat Palace Hotel* is a romantic highlight in the "city of eternal spring." For a more informal evening, try the Cellar Bar, which serves hearty European food daily.

Special recommendations

A cool draft beer in the Cellar Bar of the legendary *Dalat Palace*. You may meet the most thoroughly French representative of the hotel – its General Manager, Antoine Sirot, in beret and cardigan. Monsieur Sirot knows Dalat better than anyone. A tour of the city in his 1929 Citroën is an unforgettable experience.

Information

Golf *Dalat Palace Golfclub*, 12 Tran Phu St., Dalat.
Tel: 0084-863825444, fax: 0084-863825666,
e-mail: sales@vietnamgolfresorts.com,
www.vietnamgolfresorts.com

From the Highlands to the Coast

Mui Ne – The South Coast

A total eclipse opens the eyes: in 1995 people from all over the world met on the beach at Mui Ne to watch the eclipse of the decade. But in the darkness, some saw even more – a vacation paradise of the future.

Au revoir, Dalat, merci, Antoine, xin chao, Mr. Lai. Vietnam's history is shaped by comings and goings. But driving – or being driven – is the stuff of great stories. Horror stories, adventure stories, stories without an end. Don't miss the opportunity to create your own stories by hiring a car and driver for longer, overland excursions. You should be aware that on the roads of Vietnam, the passengers' well-being depends not on the comfort of the car's seats, but on a single person: the driver. All drivers are extremely pleasant, helpful, and motivated. But there may be a few small details that grate on the nerves over a long journey. Here are a few – to be taken with a pinch of salt. The "Look out, here I come!"-type of horn honker is pretty bearable, because at least he takes a break now and again. Far worse is the "I-honk, therefore I am" honker, who never, ever, stops. Compared to these two, the cell-phone user is much easier to get on with. But the worst of all is the illegal overtaker, triggering long-lasting adrenaline attacks one after the other. Still, at least his passengers are wide awake and taking an interest in their surroundings.

My driver, Mr. Lai, has only a nodding dog and an air freshener in his car – but then so do taxi drivers in Hamburg or Munich. He likes to take notes while he telephones, which he manages fairly successfully. The crash barrier to the right of the road, the side which plunges down to the valley, looks stable enough to withstand a car and two people. He drives slowly and likes telling stories, which he does wittily. When he laughs, he pulls the car into a U-turn just as he is telling the punch line. It's really fun.

The trip from Dalat along the south coast toward Mui Ne runs through a magnificent mountainous landscape with hairpin bends aplenty. Tourism has hardy touched the southern highlands, which makes the drive all the more appealing. The south coast, and with it the busy National 1 from Saigon to Hanoi, is a mere 170 kilometers (100 miles) or so away, so that an easy, slow trip is in tune with the glorious countryside and spreads good humor. At Dai Ninh,

1 "Please run over" – a four-wheeled makeshift harvester to help thresh the rice. **2** Mud packs in hot springs by the roadside. **3** Coral bright as a paintbox. **4** Di Linh Highlands – paradise for hikers.

1 Kitesurfers on the beach of the Sailing Club at Mui Ne. **2** The dunes of Mui Ne – a natural wonder, a photographer's dream. **3** Fishers' temple at Mui Ne, where wives pray for their husbands. **4** "Safe return" – fishing boats sail out. **5** Sailing Club at Mui Ne.

the Gougar Falls beckon, and around 30 kilometers (20 miles) further, in the area of Di Linh, are extensive tea plantations founded by the French which still form the main source of revenue for the region today. Continue along the secondary road 28 toward Phan Thiet, unless blasting operations are going on for the new access road to the mountain rain forests in the Di Linh Highlands – a remote area that today offers stunning excursions for nature-loving travelers.

The hairpin bends grow fewer, and we begin to descend from the highlands to the coast. The afternoon sun bathes the plains in warm colors. Is that the sea we can smell already? In Ba Tu we turn left, shortly afterwards crossing the main Saigon-to-Hanoi railway line, and approach the sand dunes of Mui Ne. The tiny fishing village is set in a desert landscape of dunes around 30 (100 feet) meters high which glow at sunset in a vibrant reddish yellow. Of course, clambering around – on all fours – in the dunes is all part of the fun. The grains of sand crunching between our teeth and in the hair are actually trophies for our strenuous efforts, and something to be proud of. Anyway, an evening swim in the sea washes off the sand, returning it to its origins on the sea bed. Wherever we choose to stay, the best resorts are all right by the sea. The Sailing Club is a delightful example of a small, cozy group of bungalows, the perfect place to relax. Thatched houses are scattered through the luxuriant gardens; residents in those nearest the beach can almost dangle their feet in the sea from their terraces, and watch more energetic guests kite surfing, snorkeling, or sailing catamarans. Dunes, beach, and palm trees are an appropriate way to begin a bathing vacation on the endless beaches of the southern coast. The nearest large city, Phan Thiet, is only 15 minutes away – by Xe Om scooter.

Mui Ne – south coast

What to see

Sunset over the sand dunes at Mui Ne – ideal for relaxing and taking photos. A highlight for photography fans. Pink Stream Canyon, a reddish-brown gorge that has carved its way through the landscape over the centuries. Windsurfing beach right by the old fishing village – a natural harbor with fishermen who skillfully guide their round boats of woven bamboo. Mui Ne is one of those places which stay in the memory. By day, the harbor is packed with brightly painted fishing boats.

Where to stay

Sailing Club Mui Ne, 24 Nguyen Dinh Chieu Ham Tien, Mui Ne, Tel: 0084-62847440, e-mail: info@sailingclubvietnam.com, www.sailingclubvietnam.com

Cham Villas, Nguyen Dinh Chieu Ham Tien, Mui Ne, Tel: 0084-62741234, e-mail: reservations@chamvillas.com, www.chamvillas.com

5

Where to eat and drink

Sailing Club, Cham Villas, and the majority of the beach resorts serve excellent food in a cultivated atmosphere. However, the simple little restaurants along the beach also serve seafood specialties at reasonable prices.

Special recommendations

Water sports offers at the club resorts, where guests are looked after by Australian beach boys and their Vietnamese colleagues. Windsurfing, kitesurfing, jet skiing.
The bravest may ask the nearest fisherman for a lesson in steering the traditional, round basket boats.
Other forms of acrobatics are easy to find: thanks to the continuous strong winds in the area, a fantastic kiteboarding scene has sprung up, attracting crack kiters from all over the world and providing a highly entertaining show.

Diving, Surfing, Sailing

Nha Trang – Endless Beaches

When the Vietnamese gods were handing out the loveliest parts of the country's 3,200 kilometers (1,900 miles) of coastline, Nha Trang Bay must have called "Here!" several times over. The area boasts six kilometers (3.6 miles) of idyllic white beaches fringed with countless coconut palms.

When the sun is already beating down on Nha Trang Bay, the hardest part is over for the fishermen – but so is the best part for visitors. Late risers find nothing more than the freshly raked sand of the hotel beach, studded with loungers on which to spend a lazy day.

Most visitors see nothing of the colorful, bustling beach life at sunrise. Half an hour ago, the beach was crammed with people welcoming in the day in their own individual style, forming a cheerful community. Young men playing ball, older people deep in concentration performing their tai chi exercises, fisher families drawing in their nets. Friendly beach joggers calling "Hey, come on!," inviting us to join them. For many, it's the perfect way to start the day in a foreign country.

By now, however, there is only a scatter of limp, empty fishing nets, with a dying fish gasping for air here and there. The catch is transported to the fish market on mopeds, and the morning gymnasts head off to work. It's worth while going to the beach before sunrise to join the well-rested Vietnamese; this is a part of Vietnam which has always been the same and is likely to remain so, retaining its age-old character for the time being in the face of increasing waves of tourism. The people of Nha Trang have long-standing experience with foreign visitors, particularly the French and Americans. Perhaps that is the reason behind their casual nonchalance; they go about their daily business as they did before, now that the sale of souvenirs, dragon fruit, manicures, and massages on the beach is prohibited by the police as a potential irritation to the tourists. But perhaps the morning bustle is only a relic of colonial times, when the last emperor, Bao Dai, would mingle with the people here in the "Nice of Vietnam," taking the sea air. Of course, the last emperor also left behind him elegant holiday villas, now converted into elegant hotels by the new government. However, truly

1 Ana Mandara, the massage bungalow at the lotus pool. **2** Night fishing off Nha Trang – squid are attracted to neon light. **3** Dreaming under a canopy – deluxe villa at Ana Mandara. **4** A great start to the day – tai chi at dawn.

imperial luxury is to be found in only one hotel at Nha Trang: the spacious Ana Mandara Resort combines first-class international standards with an atmosphere that is a masterpiece of luxury and comfort. The hotel's wellness and spa facilities served as a powerful impetus for the Vietnamese tourism trade, raising the bar for new hotels. The Ana Mandara was long the best hotel in Vietnam, and is still one of the finest in the world. His Majesty would have reveled in it, a source of joy in his so thoroughly "stressful" existence. It is the only hotel in Nha Trang which is located on the sea and has a beach directly at its terrace; the beach, however, is open to all, for there are no private beaches in Vietnam.

On the opposite side of the Tran Phu riverbank promenade, one hotel after another has been hastily erected between the old villas, giving the coastline a somewhat "Costa Brava" charm. Fortunately, this cliché does not apply to Nha Trang. The friendly town and its environs have far more to offer. Diehard water rats and sun worshippers will find exactly what they're looking for. Attractions such as diving, jet skiing, and boat trips to the small islets in the area are enticing, and unique in Vietnam in this form. Nightlife is also varied, with plenty of choice from bars to dance floors. Tolerance is part of daily life in Vietnam, and there are special grounds for this in Nha Trang.

The coast here is the meeting point of three cultures, whose coexistence has for centuries been intimately intertwined with the development of the region's population. An enormous statue of Buddha sits at Long Son Pagoda. The bell tower of the Catholic cathedral is impossible to overlook. And the temples of Po Nagar stand on the River Cai, stone witnesses to the ancient Cham culture. This juxtaposition of philosophies is probably the reason for this tolerant coexistence, although it has not always functioned smoothly. The Buddhist monks of the 1960s who set fire to themselves in protest at the Saigon regime of the Catholic dictator Diem were from Central Vietnam, some actually from Nha Trang.

In Vietnam, history is omnipresent. Recent history is often the inspiration of reflection, while more ancient history is a feast for the curious, especially here on the south coast, which was the domicile of the Cham people until the 14th century.

Even visitors who profess to be unimpressed by old ruins end up

1 The beach is raked every morning. **2** Testing the waters. **3** Room with a view. **4** Perfect peace. **5** Bathroom in the luxury villa.

at a Cham tower sooner or later. At Phan Rang, for example, only a few kilometers from Nha Trang, this mysterious people established the center of their kingdom, Panduranga. It is the most important temple from their culture, and the Po Klong Garai complex was the best preserved of all.

Mr. Duncan's problems, however, are firmly in the here and now. As closed as a clamshell, the director of Sunrise Beach Hotel muses until he has the perfect idea: he will plan a boat trip for his guests to visit the pearl farm on the islands off Nha Trang. First of all the hotel staff must test the tour, and so he organizes a staff outing to the pearl farm in Van Phong Bay.

This bay is far and away the most beautiful in Vietnam, and is regarded as a top-quality ecological paradise for divers. A host of rules and regulations were drawn up to preserve the environment; no boat was allowed to moor without permission, and at sunset all boats had to leave the bay. Now hesitant attempts are emerging to tolerate "green tourism" – considered by experts to be the only way to preserve one of the deepest bays in the world, with its turquoise waters and sensitive coral reefs, enabling it to develop into a visitor attraction without compromising the habitats of hundreds of species of flora and fauna.

The excursion sets off. A fast speedboat and 15 jolly, motivated members of staff from the hotel head for the islands 50 kilometers (30 miles) away. All speak excellent English, and their professional smiles have been replaced by an atmosphere of genuine warmth. As always, the young people are very open and curious. They are the true pearls of Vietnam, and the finest ornament for the hotel. Their contemporaries on the rocking pontoons of the pearl farm aren't bad either. The creation of a pearl is a process which never fails to amaze those new to it; convincing nature to undertake such astonishing feats is a highly complex enterprise. For the oyster, the process is triggered by the irritation of a foreign body in its flesh, when a splinter of mother-of-pearl is carefully introduced into its shell. The oyster begins to envelop the irritating splinter in protective layers, adding a new one each year. The intruder grows in size

and slowly develops into the coveted pearl. After years of painstaking care, and assuming the oyster survives the ravages of the sea and the next typhoon, the farmer can finally harvest a precious treasure.

The evening is the perfect time for a stroll or a cyclo tour. Even Nha Trang, Vietnam's oldest seaside resort, has a few rickshaw drivers who know the old quarter like the back of their hand. However, how much longer this will continue is a moot point; the drivers are already tending to encounter brand-new houses on corners where they still expected to see old villas, confused and muttering "But I'm sure, mister, I'm really sure." In the face of such tragedy, it's best to show sympathy and give in to their outrageous fare demands.

1 Sunrise at the pearl of the beach – Sunrise Hotel, Nha Trang. **2** A rough exterior concealing precious pearls. **3** Clear water and plenty of attention – oyster farm at Van Phong Bay. **4** How does the pearl get into the oyster? **5** The true "pearls" of the hotel – its staff, on an excursion to the oyster farm.

Nha Trang – Endless Beaches

What to see

The fishing port of Nha Trang is one of the most colorful on the coast. The Buddha statue at the Catholic church and the towers of the ancient Cham people are testimonies to peaceful coexistence. The *temples of Po Nagar* are the most important remains of the lost Cham culture.

Where to stay

Ana Mandara, Six Senses Resorts & Spas, Beachside Tran Phu Blvd., Nha Trang. The beautiful boutique hotel is the only one to have direct beach access. Its delightful design features wooden interiors and rattan furnishings.
Tel: 0084-58522222, e-mail: PR-anamandara@evason-resorts.com, www.sixsenses.com
Sunrise Beach Resort, 12–14 Tran Phu Blvd., Nha Trang. Modern hotel with first-class service and probably the largest reception lobby in Vietnam, plus a trendy bar.
Tel: 0084-858820999, e-mail: info@sunrisenhatrang.com.vn, www.sunrisenhatrang.com.vn

Where to eat and drink

The selection of restaurants and bars in Nha Trang is extensive thanks to the resort's long tourist tradition. Tran Phu

riverbank promenade has the best restaurants, serving international cuisine and outstanding regional specialties. Fish and seafood restaurants are located in the center at Phan Chu Trinh. There are reasonably priced restaurants and snack bars on the beach serving superb food. Spaghetti fans should visit Signor Mai.
City Pizza Little Italy, 24A Hung Vuong St., Nha Trang.
Tel: 0084-58521893, e-mail: mailenguyen2001@yahoo.com

Special recommendations

Watching beach life at sunset is a wonderful way to learn about Vietnamese life. Van Phong Bay, with its pearl farms and underwater reefs, is one of Vietnam's most beautiful bays. Nightlife offers everything a tourist's heart desires – all night long.

Information

Exotissimo Travel Vietnam Co Ltd, Saigon Finance Center
9 Dinh Tien Hoang, District 1, *Ho-Chi-Minh-City.*
Tel: 008488251723-283, e-mail: infoEXO@exotissimo.com
go.vietnam@exotissimo.com,
www.exotissimo.com

The Challenge of Concealment

Ninh Van Bay – Bay of Rediscovered Senses

Rediscovering the senses – don't we all dream of that in today's fast-paced world? And yet many people find that one of the greatest challenges is to reawaken their senses, dulled by computers, cellphones, and the Internet.

The "journey to the lost senses" starts on the way from Cam Ranh Airport to Nha Trang. The driver controls the elegant vehicle with its tinted windows with caution and mastery. A charming hostess offers fresh fruit and bottled water in an appetizing linen "apron" – true, it conceals nothing more than the Vietnamese brand of water "La Vie," but adds a touch of sensuous style to our everyday routine. As our ears are caressed by classical music, we can feel that our willingness to abandon ourselves to gentle, sensuous pleasures is already unfolding.

Check-in is completed in the little reception area for boat transfers to the remote bay. From this point onward, all the customary difficulties of getting around in a foreign country are history. The snow-white overalls of the "Senses Team" indicate to us that the time has come to bid farewell to the world of stress. And it works. In a fast motorboat, we embark on the 30-minute journey to Ninh Van Bay and rapidly shake off all our bad moods.

Ninh Van Bay is smaller, more tranquil, and more attractive than we expected, with whiter sand and higher mountains as a backdrop. After the engine of the boat is switched off, stillness reigns. Even the waves lap silently. Not a hotel in sight. The endless jetty up to the beach looks like the last link to the outside world.

One brief glance back, then we pass through a glorious tropical garden bright with lush greenery and colorful flowers. Bees busily collect nectar, and butterflies dance around the new arrival.

Only a few meters further on, our personal butler, male or female, enters the idyll. From now on, he or she will take care of everything which could distract us from our personal process of reawakening.

The rustic bungalows of natural stone and wood, reminiscent of traditional Vietnamese forms, are equipped with every possible convenience. They have a simple bedroom and a living area on the upper floor, open on all sides and shaded with wooden blinds, between which our gaze passes over the palm tree crowns to the

1 Massage oil for the skin. **2** Caresses for the soul. **3** Concentrating on essentials. **4** Evason Hideaway, Rock Villa – the ultimate in relaxation.

1 Beach villa with its own pool at Evason Hideaway. **2** Open sleeping veranda with sea view. **3** Open-air bathroom in Rock Villa. **4** Zen garden and path to the top spa on the hill. **5** Exclusively for guests – the jetty at Evason Hideaway.

sea. It creates an immediate feeling of oneness with nature – whether we like it or not. Initially, we have the feeling of being at the mercy of our surroundings, defenseless. But soon the room becomes our preferred place to sleep instead of the bedroom downstairs. A place to dream under palms and the starry tropical sky.

Five bungalows perch here on the bare rocks amid the sea; at first glance they convey an atmosphere reminiscent of monastic strictness that promises only ascetic simplicity. Yet this impression is followed by the sybaritic life of a kind of luxury hermit, watching fishermen at work while basking in the bath. There is a special charm to the penance we are about to pay for our maltreated senses.

For this reason, the daily shuttle boat to the vibrant, lively riverbank promenade at Nha Trang is generally empty. Our personal butler at

Evason Hideaway has a daily roster of attractive pastimes on offer, ranging from tennis, water sports and diving, workouts and gymnastics, to trekking, river trips, mountain excursions – or simply chilling.

Many stressed managers and seekers of the meaning of life select the option of simply doing nothing. A difficult task, and one which requires practice. Our approach to the inner self is helped along by Japanese Zen-style gardens, waterfalls, scent gardens, and open-air massages. Long walks along the beach are less appealing, since the bay offers only a kilometer of sand for the purpose; what we discover here is the space to let the senses unfold. After a few days, this space expands to become immeasurably large.

Ninh Van Bay to the south enjoys 250 days of sunshine per year, with temperatures ranging from 26 to 34 degrees Celsius. Hermits who miss their glorious sunrises can sail into the sun at dawn in a fishing boat. The sturdy boats can moor at the long jetty. We can take advantage of this romantic, early morning trip to select the fish for our evening dinner – there's nothing fresher and heartier.

Ninh Van Bay – Bay of Reawakened Senses

What to see

Evason Hideaway Resort, with its white beaches and mountains, is itself worth seeing. To gain a bigger picture of the region, hike along the headland of the peninsula. Nature lovers can observe the wildlife of the area in tranquility, on tours conducted by an expert native guide.

Where to stay

Evason Hideaway & Six Senses Spa at Ana Mandara
The resort comprises several detached villas located on the beach, in the forest, and on the rocky coast in the sea. Inspired by traditional Vietnamese architecture, they are furnished in natural materials, in a combination of luxury and nature which captures the resort's philosophy. A fitness center, library, and several bars are perfect for relaxation, offering heavenly views of the private bay and the sea with adjoining rain forest.
Evason Hideaway & Six Senses Spa at Ana Mandara, Ninh Van Bay, Ninh Hoa, Khanh Hoa, Tel: 0084-58524268, e-mail: reservations-anamandara@evasonhideaways.com

Where to eat and drink

The restaurant at the resort is outstanding and will fulfill every desire, with an overwhelming choice of fresh fruits and freshly pressed juices.

Special recommendation

Take a journey to find yourself and rediscover your senses in the fabulous spa and wellness center of *Evason Hideaway Resort*.

Information

Exotissimo Travel Vietnam Co Ltd, Saigon Finance Center
9 Dinh Tien Hoang, District 1, *Ho-Chi-Minh-City.*
Tel: 008488251723-283,
e-mail: infoEXO@exotissimo.com,
go.vietnam@exotissimo.com,
www.exotissimo.com

Headwind and 18 Holes

Phan Thiet – Golf Course and Surfing Paradise

When winds get up to gale force six or seven,
some pack up – while others are only just starting.
What's too stormy for the 9th hole is just warming up
for the downride along the coast from Mui Ne to Phan Thiet!

Along the 15 kilometers (9 miles) of beach between Mui Ne and Phan Thiet two worlds of tourism meet that could hardly offer more extreme contrasts. Golfers and surfers peacefully coexist here in their common paradise – the golfers since 1995, the surfers since 2000.

The Ocean Dunes golf course may not be quite what the exclusive greens at Dalat have in mind, but some lighthearted jockeying is at stake here. "Who's the loveliest in the land?" is the question. There's no doubt that the 9th hole is certainly the most beautiful in the whole of Vietnam, and it's among the world's top 500. The magnificent green is on a small hill close to the sea. Golfing superstar Nick Faldo, who designed the course, describes it as the loveliest beach golf course in the world.

Superlatives like these also tumble from the lips of international kiting and windsurfing cracks when they describe the 15-kilometer (9 mile) beach between the headland at Mui Ne and the harbor at Phan Thiet. It's quite simply a top surfing paradise that is well able to compete with all other idyllic Asian surfing locations. But the two sports represented here, golf and surfing, never conflict. When one starts, the other has to stop. Such is the natural law in these sports; this coastline location is permanently windy, and occasionally play is impossible – particularly at the 9th hole. Yet these conditions offer just the kind of challenge that surfers love most. They rip along the coast with a strong but steady wind at their backs. The wind blows "onshore," from the sea to the coastline, a continuous fresh breeze that enables the surfers to make steady progress from Mui Ne to the beach at Phan Thiet and land up directly in front of Novotel Coralia and the Ocean Dunes Golf Club. They don't bother anyone; quite the opposite, in fact – it's a fantastic sight to see up to 50 kitesurfers scudding over the powerful waves in the late afternoon when the sun is low, and reining in their brightly colored sails on the beach in front of the hotel.

1 At Ocean Dunes Golf Club – one of the loveliest beach golf courses in the world. **2** Marguerite the cow going about her work. **3** Preparations for the sun worshippers. **4** Traditional life is not about to disappear – the jet skis will soon be gone.

By that time, the golfers are already sitting in the bar of the golf club and looking forward to the next windless morning. You see, in an attempt to please both the "wild bunch" of surfers and the more dignified golfers, the wind never rises before 9 a.m, only getting up speed around 2 p.m. and leaving plenty of time for a nine-hole round before letting rip once again in the afternoon.

At the start of the golfing season over a decade ago, the fishing town of Phan Thiet attracted few visitors. Even today it is not crowded. The little harbor has retained its traditional air, and it's fun to sail through the narrow entrance when returning from a trip on a fishing boat. The fishermen are serene, relaxed characters and very entertaining, making up for their less than fluent English with voluble gestures – particularly when they demonstrate their brilliant maneuvering skills between buoys, police boats, and their colleagues in their unstable woven coracles. In this variation of "Battleships," the fisher steers his boat with one foot – a pretty cool move that needs strong nerves. When your hands are shaking, it's hard to clamber over the three other boats sharing the quayside mooring with our bold buccaneer.

The fish market at Phan Thiet is around the corner. No need to ask directions – the scent is better than any sat-nav system. It's the fresh shellfish that smell so strongly, say some. No, it's the *nuoc*

1 Seven in the morning when tourists are still asleep – the unique fish market at Phan Thiet is wide awake. **2** Family affair – everyone joins in. **3** Round and round – the fishermen's paddle boats. **4** The 9th hole – a golfer's beachside paradise.

mam, say others, adding that the fish sauce from Phan Thiet is naturally much better than the one from the island of Phu Quoc. And if the intensity of the smell is anything to go by, they might be right. The town center is delightful, allowing visitors to stroll undisturbed through the little stores and watch the Vietnamese going about their daily business. What they buy, how they haggle, how they behave with each other. Street restaurants serve fresh fish, and the battle cry of money, "Tien, Tien, Tien," a declaration of war on tourists' wallets, is not yet all-pervasive. You're more likely to hear "Hey, mister! Yesterday you paid too much for your pictures." This from the man in the photo store, grinning and waving a 100,000 dong note, which now finds its way back into the happy tourist's pocket.

Phan Thiet – Golf Course and Surfing Paradise

What to see
The traditional fish market at Phan Thiet with its blue and white boats. The starting and landing beaches of the international kitesurfing community; they start at Mui Ne and surf to Phan Thiet. The beautiful golf course of Ocean Dunes, also a delightful walk for non-golfers. The charming, little old quarter on the River Ca Ty.

Where to stay
Novotel Coralia Ocean Dunes Resort, 1 Ton Duc Thang St., Phan Thiet. Tel: 0084-62822393,
e-mail: novpht@hcm.vnn.vn,
www.accorhotels-asia.com/asia

Where to eat and drink
Phan Thiet has only few restaurants, but they are excellent; for example, *Nam Thanh Lau* serves *lau*, the famous fish hotpot. There is only one problem: if the wind is in the wrong direction, the smell of the fish sauce factories can impair dining pleasure. Far from this undesirable fragrance, the *Sea Horse Restaurant* at the Novotel serves tuna, swordfish or scampi in an elegant atmosphere with a view of the beach.

Special recommendations
Take an early morning trip on a fishing boat when the nets are brought in; for some morning gymnastics, help with the pulling. The *Ho Chi Minh Museum* on the banks of the River Ca Ty examines the early life of the freedom fighter.

4

Information
Golf Ocean Dunes Golfclub, 1 Ton Duc Thang St., Phan Thiet.
Tel: 0084-62822393, e-mail: novpht@hcm.vnn.vn,
www.accorhotels-asia.com/asia
Exotissimo Travel Vietnam Co Ltd, Saigon Finance Center
9 Dinh Tien Hoang, District 1, *Ho-Chi-Minh-City.*
Tel: 0084-88251723-283,
e-mail: infoEXO@exotissimo.com,
go.vietnam@exotissimo.com,
www.exotissimo.com

Time Out for Body and Soul

Quy Nhon – Tai Chi and Yoga

"It is a voracious joy and causes a delightful intoxication
to illuminate the collection of my memory.
The landscapes I passed through
have the poisoned beauty of a flower of passion."

Han Mac Tu was a famous writer of romantic poems in Vietnam in the first half of the 20th century. Admired for the beauty and clarity of his poetry, the handsome young man is unforgotten for his tragic fate: he died of leprosy at the age of only 28. Han Mac Tu was buried near Quy Nhon. His poetry lives on, imbued with a mystical purity through his untimely death. Some of his poems have become reflective songs, describing how we can draw a wonderful energy from the deepest recesses of our innermost being, for only peace of heart can become a new source of strength.

But how can we find peace and strength on a journey packed with experiences, where all the senses are constantly occupied with new impressions? There is one possibility, which we can learn from the Vietnamese: switch off, simply switch off, in the center of the city, in a park, at the river, by the lake, on the beach. All it takes is a little practice and some basic knowledge of the most popular form of exercise here: tai chi. This particularly subtle form of meditative whole-body training aims at relaxing the muscles to release new energy. Westerners have some initial difficulties when faced with the idea of opening up one's inner recesses in public. They feel uncomfortable and clumsy when performing tai chi exercises, and try to master the slowness of the movements at top speed. But when we have overcome these initial vanities and the ingrained compulsion of Westerners to succeed, our external environment shrinks to a bare minimum, we begin to focus on our own ego, and our journey into our inner being has begun.

The point at which to plan this heady adventure may prove to be a purely geographical consideration determined by the route one selects at the beginning. Perhaps it is the final act before returning home, or a pause before continuing to travel north. Whatever the reason, our starting point for the journey within is almost exactly in the center of Vietnam.

1 Sewing lesson in the neighboring village. **2** Enchanting blossoms in a wooden tub. **3** Hot sand to soothe stressed souls – a sweat bath in the quartz sauna. **4** Harmony of body and soul – hard rocks, soft sand, rolling ocean – the perfect place for tai chi.

1 To begin with, let both hands drift upward. **2** Put the weight on the back foot, draw back, and push the hands forward while breathing out. **3** Move the arms sideways, with the backs of the hands towards the body. **4** Move the hands away from the body in a circular movement. **5** Onto the mat before breakfast – yoga at sunrise. **6** Relaxing the hips – the "butterfly" lotus position.

To most people, Quy Nhon is no more than an insignificant little fishing village on Vietnam's extensive southern coast, around 230 kilometers (140 miles) from Nha Trang and around 350 kilometers (210 miles) from Hoi An. The better-known destinations have generally taken precedence in tourists' travel plans, enticing visitors with sun, sand, and culture and outshining the pretty village of Quy Nhon.

This has now changed. Quy Nhon is the ideal spot to break the long journey from one famous destination to the other, between South and Central Vietnam. It's the perfect location in which to enjoy a few days of time out in absolute peace and tranquility. And this was the idea behind Quy Nhon Life Resort, established in the secluded bay with its two beaches and rugged crags. The resort specializes exclusively in peace and contemplation, achieved through tai chi and yoga. While its philosophical inspiration and metaphorical architect was the teaching of *feng shui* ("wind and water"), its actual builder is Louk Lennaerts, a Dutchman who has lived in Vietnam for ten years and has consistently put into action his personal experiences of the Asian way of life. As Louk says, "Asian wisdom: we need only observe heaven and earth in order to win the favor of the *feng shui*, the spirits of the air and water. And that's what I did."

The result is an architecture of well-defined forms and lines, flowing harmoniously into the gently curving arches of the Cham temples. An architectural homage to the lost people of the Cham, who flourished for centuries in the region around Quy Nhon.

If we are prepared to absorb this atmosphere with awareness, we can already note its first effects on us as we cross the entrance and the open hall. The flames of the petroleum lamps flicker in the

breeze and an unceasing stream of water trickles along a narrow marble channel, its sharply delineated sides meeting at the horizon and uniting in eternity. The effect is of a promise. Here, at this very spot, body and soul can come together again.

The daily program includes tai chi, meditation, and yoga courses from the resort's 16 trainers. Four and six-hand massages dispel the last remnants of stiffness from travel-weary bodies and the bravest volunteer immediately for "burial."

The Quartz Sand Sauna is a hit with health-conscious guests. The ultra-fine, snow-white sand it uses is found at only one place in Vietnam, in the region of Cam Ranh, not far from Nha Trang. Here it is excavated and shipped all over the world; we encounter it in egg-timers, or – after the sand sauna – in our mouth, nose, and ears. After the sauna, a blossom oil bath is the perfect way to cleanse body and soul. And that's all we can do for the time being. A light fish dinner, the catch of the day from the neighboring fishing village, rounds off our inner journey for the night.

1 A masterful symbiosis of old and new – the entrance to Life Resort Quy Nhon. **2** Feng shui – Chinese garden art to soothe guests and ghosts. **3** For two hearts and souls in perfect harmony – a romantic bath of love, with scented blossoms and candlelight. **4** Idyllic bay with pool and beach.

From six o'clock the next morning we can consider whether to prioritize awakening our senses or ourselves. The first alternative involves yoga, the second – as usual – coffee, taken in the delightful open restaurant. But however appealing the atmosphere here, at some point the faint roar of nearby Freeway Number 1 beckons. Its brand-new, extra-wide asphalt simply begs us to explore. Our route is quickly organized; the friendly receptionists are familiar with the turbulent energies of their well-rested guests. The twelve kilometers (6.5 miles) into the town are quickly behind us, and on the last section of the new road the landscape before Quy Nhon unfolds before us once again, as if to remind us who the boss is around here. The view from the hill on the peninsula is breathtaking, with untouched beaches stretching almost to the town. Here, normal day-to-day life pays no heed to inquisitive visitors. Normality in this city is an event in itself.

At the beach, directly opposite the only state-run luxury hotel, the fishermen of Quy Nhon land their catch. The bulging nets and bewildering variety of fish and seafood are the most impressive in all our journey so far – as is the fact that the fishermen cook their catch right next to their boats.

The profound effects of the tai chi and yoga exercises are transformed into a source of energy, enabling us to overcome our innate hesitancy born of civilization. "Long-noses" are naturally welcomed, and the whole clan assembles skewers wrapped in leaves for the foreign visitors. Green tea is served at a "flat rate" – unlimited tea, but also unlimited ice. It becomes one of our most delightful afternoons on the southern coast. Amid the tumult on the

beach and the roar of traffic and chorus of car horns from the nearby freeway, the motley group around their steaming cooking pots forms a small but impregnable island. And strangely enough, our gut feelings of happiness and contentment are similar to those experienced after tai chi or yoga.

The hectic, colorful market a few streets away entices us; a nearby "Off Limits!" sign reawakens the past of this sleepy little town. The outskirts of the harbor, a military restricted zone, remind us that Quy Nhon was once one of the four largest US marine bases, together with Da Nang, Nha Trang, and Cam Ranh Bay. Eco-tours through the province of Binh Dinh are more appealing. Families of potters and rice-paper manufacturers genially reveal their trade secrets. Tay Son Museum has lost its attraction, but the evening tai chi exercises between the sea crags have become a regular activity on our agenda for discovering peace of mind and the energy which flows from it.

Quy Nhon – Tai Chi and Yoga

What to see
The twin towers at *Thap Doi*, built by the Cham people. Not far from here was the religious and political center of their kingdom of Champa, with its northern capital of Vijaya. For this reason, many ancient remains of the once-powerful Cham can still be found in the region. There is a small but not particularly beautiful museum, *Binh Dinh* at Nguyen Hue, with some interesting exhibits.

Where to stay
Life Resort Quy Nhon, Ghenh Rang, Bai Dai Beach, Quy Nhon. Tel: 0084-56840132,
e-mail: quynhon@life-resorts.com, www.life-resorts.com

Where to eat and drink
Don't be wet – try a frog. Deliciously roasted and exquisitely flavored at *Que Huong* 2, 185 Le Hong Phong. The choice of seafood at the *Life Resort* restaurant is also pretty good. The day's catch, fresh from the traps, is displayed so appetizingly that it's irresistible. The head chef comes over in person to discuss diners' preferences. A feast for the palate and the soul.

4

Special recommendations
The most attractive view of the peninsula can be seen from a hill along the new freeway. A hands-on visit to the harbor is also fascinating. The beach is the fishermen's province, where the fresh catch is spread out, and the women set up countless cooking fires to feed their hungry captains and sailors after a long night at sea. Visitors are welcome to try the freshest fish around.

Information
Life Resorts Development, Louk Lennaerts, 64/28 Pho Quang St., Ho-Chi-Minh-City. Tel: 0084-82969883,
e-mail: Lennaerts@life-resorts.com,
www.resort-creations.com
Exotissimo Travel Vietnam Co Ltd, Saigon Finance Center
9 Dinh Tien Hoang, District 1, *Ho-Chi-Minh-City.*
Tel: 0084-88251723-283,
e-mail: infoEXO@exotissimo.com,
go.vietnam@exotissimo.com,
www.exotissimo.com

From Tower to Tower

The Secret of the Cham Towers

A place of honor for the gods.
Channels for the blood from the sacrifices.
Three floors of the wisdom of life.
The holy towers of the Cham – witnesses to a mysterious culture.

Five towers back, five towers on the spot, six towers forward. The logical formula to accompany a journey leading from Cham tower to Cham tower between Quy Nhon and Central Vietnam.

Today home to some of Vietnam's most beautiful vacation destinations, this coastline was once the site of the great kingdom of Champa, which flourished here for over 1,400 years. It was founded by that legendary people who were forced to fight for their independence throughout their entire history, rather like the Vietnamese in the last hundred years. Yet this historical similarity does not give rise to common ground of any significance for coexistence today. As we journey from tower to tower, we can picture the dimensions of the Cham kingdom at its zenith and imagine what it was like to be constantly compelled to defend the fertile land. In its heyday, the kingdom once stretched from the Mekong Delta in the south to Dong Hoi in the north.

Shipping in the South China Sea, the traditional spice trade, and skills in wetland rice cultivation laid the financial foundations for the Cham people's rapid economic expansion in this fertile coastal region. This attracted not only trading partners who came in peace, but also robbers and the envious. In addition, the Cham's religious and cultural habits seem to have been at odds with the region. Cham beliefs encompassed the migration of souls and shamans, Hindu, and Buddhist features from India. The greatest figure in their philosophy was the Hindu god Shiva, the ruler of all things earthly. So it was that over a millennium ago, the Cham people built the temples of Po Nagar, also in Shiva's honor. This brought the Khmer into the equation, triggering an endless battle for power in Indochina. The Cham were long incapable of standing up to these fierce attacks. In the 14th century they still put up feeble resistance, but by the 15th century the Cham had finally been defeated, the remnants of their proud kingdom destroyed by the

1 The most beautiful Cham towers at Phan Rang. **2** Guardian and snake charmer – the guard at My Son. **3** 3,000 years of culture close enough to touch – the Cham Museum at Da Nang. **4** More than 70 temples, the remains of a great culture – My Son.

lords of Hue. Since those times, many a ruin has lain moldering under a carpeting of rampant jungle; only the old shrine of My Son has been excavated. But the towers of the Cham still rear proudly over the landscape, as if striving desperately to bear testimony to the great kingdom to which these mighty monuments once belonged.

Many are still in good condition and can be safely viewed. Some are encased in bamboo scaffolding and are undergoing extensive renovation. It is interesting to see the plans, unrolled by the Vietnamese restoration team; they give a clear picture of how the towers once looked and how much was recreated. The restorers are skilful in using similar techniques to those practised by the ancient Cham, although they have still to solve the problem of how to join the bricks without using mortar. Some suspect that tree resin was used as a kind of early superglue. No hints are given as to how today's restorers solve this problem.

The highlights of this journey from tower to tower are definitely the valley of My Son and the Cham Museum at Da Nang. They convey a comprehensive picture of this lost culture, which, despite

the discovery of many informative artifacts and a now-deciphered script, leaves us with many unanswered questions and a host of mysteries.

The temple city of My Son is easy to reach from Hoi An. However, to be truly swept away by the magic of the ruins, avoid the early

morning bus. The afternoon bus is a better choice, and it is definitely worthwhile hiring a good guide and driver. The staff at My Son are certainly more relaxed when the rush hour is over, and can be persuaded to make small concessions, allowing visitors to climb behind barriers or onto walls to snap the ultimate panoramic shot – digital or analog. The dollar is the going currency.

The exhibition hall houses some outstanding Cham sculptures, but also some rusting grenade casings. In their desperation and rage at the Vietcong, who had hidden in the ruins at My Son, the US forces practically carpeted the valley with bombs. Parts of the temples were blown to bits in days – but the Vietcong continued to fight. If prestigious academics all over the world had not rushed to intervene with the US president, the rest would also have been razed. Today, the ruins of the ruins are under UNESCO protection as a cultural monument – and the grenade casings stand among the sculptures as a warning.

1 Heritage of the Cham culture – restorations at Phan Rang. **2** Indian mythology – the Cham Museum. **3** The mysterious script of the Cham. **4** Rainy season – time for culture, the Cham Museum at Da Nang.

The Secrets of the Cham Towers

What to see

The most extensive, and thus the most informative, remains of the Cham culture between Quy Nhon and Da Nang can be seen in the *temple city of My Son*. A tour of these ruins gives a clear impression of the former might of this kingdom. A useful conclusion to this chapter of Vietnam's long history is a visit to the excellent *Cham Museum* at Da Nang. This internationally acclaimed exhibition has also toured abroad several times, most recently to Paris.

Where to stay

Overnight accommodation is not necessary for this day excursion along the well-developed A1 freeway. Even with plenty of stops for photography and rests, the trip takes around six hours.

4

Where to eat and drink

The best solution is to trust the tour guide and driver; the team always has snacks ready to appease hunger pangs en route. Those who prefer to eat in comfort will find plenty of restaurants on the way. But don't be deceived by the size of the restaurants. Here, as so often, the maxim "less is more" applies. The customer is king in the small, family-run restaurants.

Special recommendation (or perhaps not)

My Lay: the site of the worst massacre in the history of the Vietnam War, on March 16, 1968. The memorial park has become a place of tranquility, with little trace of the propaganda of retribution. Let your personal feelings decide whether you make the visit.

Information

It is also possible to fly from *Quy Nhon* to *Da Nang*. The Cham towers at My Son are within easy reach of Da Nang or Hoi An. There are three flights per week from Quy Nhon and daily flights to Saigon. Vietnam Airlines, 2 Duong Ly Thuong Kiet 056823125.

Moonlight festival at Hoi An, with poetry, lamps and song. Once a month, the city is filled with poetic enchantment.

The Middle Kingdom

Three Places Steeped in History – Da Nang, Hoi An, Hue

ĐỘNG HUYỀN KHÔNG
ĐỘNG HOA NGHIÊM
ĐỘNG LINH NHAM
ĐỘNG TÀNG CHƠN
TAM TÔN ĐƯỜNG
CHÙA TAM THAI
CHÙA LINH ỨNG
GIANG ĐÀI
NHÀ PHƯƠNG TRƯỢNG
VỌNG HẢI ĐÀI
ĐỘNG VÂN THÔNG
ĐƯỜNG VÀO A
ĐƯỜNG VÀO B
1
2
3
4

Love at Second Sight

Da Nang – Central Vietnam

Occasionally, when we open our minds to banal things and abandon all expectations, we may suddenly gain unexpected insights and broad perspectives of Vietnamese daily life in the country's third-largest port.

"That way," says the elderly man at Da Nang airport, pointing to the city. "The best market is on the river, that's where life's happening." Mr. Thien knows what he's talking about. Just stay here, he advises, and don't bother heading off to the tourist traps at Hoi An and Hue. Day-to-day life in his Vietnamese hometown also has its charms. Okay then, Mr. Thien – we'll postpone the Marble Mountains, the Cham Museum, China Beach, and Furama Hotel. But now explain to us where you learnt your good English and your smattering of German! Nguyen van Thien was a motorcycle courier for a long time right here in Da Nang, at what was then the largest US base, enabling him to feed his family and learn English. He learnt his German from his neighbor, who lived "behind the wall" in Germany for a long time – the 70-year-old gives a broad, knowing grin and starts up his courier bike from all those years ago, a 1964 scooter which he succeeded in hiding on March 29, 1975, when the North Vietnamese invaded. Thien subsequently had to take an intensive course, in Vietnamese, to learn the alphabet of the new regime in Hanoi.

Mr. Thien is part of the city's history, which has awakened to new life: liberal, colorful, open, and with a vibrant international business sector. Foreigners can move through the streets without being plagued by "Hey, mister!" calls, and enjoy the bustle of the markets and the old quarter. The long riverbank promenade beckons to us for a stroll, fringed by restaurant boats and hotels. Bach Dang Hotel is the most pleasant. Though not a new building and still exuding a kind of socialist charm, the staff are extremely kind and there is a fascinating view of the Han River. Everywhere is within walking distance, although a flock of classic cyclos stands in front of the hotel. The drivers are reliable and open to individual arrangements – such as a visit to Cham Museum, as a kind of conclusion to the in-depth exploration of this culture. The French established the museum in 1916 in a villa on the Han River, assembling

1 Paths to the five Marble Mountains. **2** Peaceful conquest, China Beach belongs to the schoolchildren. **3** Baywatch in Vietnamese for swimmers and surfers. **4** Face to face forty years ago – US bunker and Vietcong hideout: China Beach and the Marble Mountains.

Vietnam's most comprehensive exhibition of Cham art from the 4th to the 12th centuries.

On the other side of the river loom Moc, Hoa, Thoa, Kim, and Thuy – the Marble Mountains named for the five basic elements in the Chinese teaching of the creation of the world: wood, fire, earth, metal, and water. According to legend, a dragon hatched from its egg at this spot, the fragments of eggshell becoming the mountains. The rock formations and surrounding landscape are even more impressive when viewed from 100 meters (330 feet) further up. Over one thousand worn stone steps wait to be ascended. Halfway up, near Tham Thai monastery, is a resting place. Only a short distance onward, climbers are rewarded with a magnificent view across the South China Sea and the other four Marble Mountains. Almost invisible chasms lead into the heart of the rock. Caves yawn, some gigantic in size; the largest is Huyen Kong Cave, with Buddhist shrines. Once a day the sun's rays fall through cavities in the rock to create a dramatic lighting effect.

Stonemasons hammer and saw away at the foot of the mountains, forming often idiosyncratic creations aimed not only at

Da Nang – Central Vietnam

What to see
The long waterside promenade at *Bach Dang*, with early morning gymnasts and tai chi disciples. Main *Han Market* on the Han River. *Cham Museum* in the old French villa near the Han River. *Cao Dai* Temple, 63 Hai Phong; in second place behind Thay Ninh Temple for national importance.

Where to stay
Furama Resort Danang, 68 Ho Xuan Huong St., Da Nang. Vietnam's first five-star hotel, opened in 1996. Outstanding atmosphere and extremely comfortable rooms, many of which have direct beach access. Guests can feel thoroughly safe there; the staff keeps a close eye on what goes on in the water. Tel: 0084-511847888 or 847333, e-mail: furamadn@hn.vnn.vn, www.furamavietnam.com

Bach Dang Hotel, 50 Duong Bach Dang, Da Nang. Very friendly Vietnamese business hotel with river views. Friendly cyclo drivers at the entrance who charge fair prices. Tel: 0084-511823649, e-mail: bdhotel@dng.vnn.vn

Where to eat and drink
Indochine Garden Restaurant, 18 Duong Tran Phu. Tel: 0084-511887007. Vietnamese and French cuisine in a beautifully kept garden. Insiders' tip: fresh draft Pils. Da Nang Export beer can be found in small bars at the end of Phan Chu Trinh not far from Cham Museum.

Special recommendations
A walk along China Beach, where the Marines once pursued their fitness training. An excursion to the mysterious Marble Mountains, hiking up and down the steps and from cave to cave. The Buddha factory at the foot of the mountains, where stonemasons have worked for centuries.

Information
Exotissimo Travel Vietnam Co Ltd, Saigon Finance Center 9 Dinh Tien Hoang, District 1, *Ho-Chi-Minh-City.*
Tel: 0084-88251723-283,
e-mail: infoEXO@exotissimo.com,
go.vietnam@exotissimo.com,
www.exotissimo.com

Asia Explore, 87 Nghia Thuc St.
Tel: 0084-82123133 or 9242092,
e-mail: asia-explore@vnn.vn,
www.asia-explore.vn

tourists. They have been working the white, gray, and pink marble here since the 15th century, producing fat Buddhas and slim mermaids.

My Khe, Da Nang's most famous beach, has long been reclaimed by the Vietnamese, and is now an early morning meeting place for Vietnamese sports fans. In the brilliant morning sun, the Water Rescue Department tower is momentarily reminiscent of the observation towers erected by the US military here on "China Beach" to ensure no harm would come to surfing Marines. Today, the beach has been reconquered – by schoolchildren from all over the country who come here on class excursions.

Three kilometers (2 miles) further along the same beach is Furama Resort, which became Vietnam's first luxury five-star hotel over 15 years ago. Voted Vietnam's best hotel six times, it has retained its legendary reputation to this day.

1 Asian nonchalance. **2** Furama Resort, traditionally luxurious.
3 Marble for the world, a quarry for statues of Buddha and bric-a-brac.
4 Looking through nature, holes in the rocks of the Marble Mountains.
5 A reception committee at Furama. **6** Beach apartment.

A Journey Through Time

Hoi An – 500 Years of Living History

Wherever we go in the little town of Hoi An – probably the most obviously multicultural settlement in all Vietnam – we walk between worlds, eras and cultures.

Three streets, three buildings, three hours – it's practically an indecent proposal for Vietnam's most enchantingly beautiful city. This schedule would be the shortest, and thus also the most painful, rendezvous imaginable with Hoi An, a pearl at the mouth of the Thu Bon river. Accept only if all else fails: a day and a night of undivided attention is the minimum that Hoi An deserves.

Even a fleeting visit to the Old Quarter imprints so many impressions on our mind that we immediately grasp what it is that gives the city its flair and uniqueness. On the short route between the fish market and the Japanese Bridge we move through the town's richly faceted history as if in a time machine. Every building, every temple still bears witness to its past significance for world trade between China, Japan and, later, Portugal. By recognizing Hoi An as their Asian trading center, it was principally the Chinese and Japanese who were allowed to establish special quarters with their own governing administrations. The two districts were linked by the covered Japanese Bridge, today Hoi An's unofficial landmark.

Throughout the centuries, many incomers pursuing the career of merchants and traders came to regard Hoi An as a second home. This was particularly true for the Chinese, whose close social ties and cultural life profoundly shaped the town's development. Hoi An received additional impetus in the mid-16th century when the Portuguese sailed down the Thu Bon river into its harbor. The Europeans quickly aligned themselves to the commercial alliance with the Vietnamese, and were permitted from then on by the Lords of Hue to purchase spices, herbs, oils, medicinal plants, porcelain, and silk for European markets. This last flowering of Hoi An spanned only a few generations and literally ran aground; as the river estuary silted up and became narrower, sailing ships were growing larger and soon began to anchor at the neighboring port of Da Nang, where the future offered more than a handspan of water under the keel. And thus ended an exciting era for the town of Hoi An.

1 Phuong and her girlfriend, two schoolgirls from Hoi An. **2** Fashion new and old, in "Tailors' Alley." **3** In the potters' village by Thu Bon river it's all about clay. **4** Gallery, guesthouse and food stall – dinner with a busy, lively family.

1 Making a sale is incidental – painters' gossip corner. **2** Japanese Bridge – tourists amid the daily hustle and bustle. **3** In the courtyard of the Chinese Assembly Hall. **4** The old man and the door – state your business before viewing the shrine.

Today, Hoi An's harbor is home to no more than sampans and fishing boats moored along the old quay. Most appear very early, before sunrise, unloading the night's fresh catch for sale at the fish market. It is one of Vietnam's most beautiful markets, and despite the camera-toting tourists gingerly picking their way through the slippery heaps of seafood, frogs, and crabs, it has retained its authentic charm and offers a panorama of Vietnamese life. The ebullient stall-holders are seldom irritated by the photography and filming – although they prefer to receive a questioning smile by way of asking permission, and will then pile on the charm, smoothing stray hairs out of their faces with fish-scale-caked hands. A photographer seeking to gain favour with the fishwives of Hoi An need only bring a few prints of his most successful pictures in the evening to become the number one in Hoi An – for a while.

Two streets further on we reach Tran Phu, one of three streets which unfurls the most colorful everyday life of the old quarter before tourists and natives alike. Here, the galleries of Chinese

lacquer and Vietnamese painting convey an impression of the diverse creativity of Hoi An's artists. But the most famous specialty can be seen in every possible variation in front of the open storefronts – the tailor's dummies of the "gallant little tailors." Vietnamese couturiers employ an array of fashionable variations and colors in their attempts to match the taste of the European fashion scene; they may not always be wholly successful, but they awaken a desire among tourists for new clothes and deliver bespoke garments within 24 hours.

At the end of Tran Phu is the Assembly Hall of the Cantonese Chinese, featuring the smug-looking "carp of prosperity" *Ca Chep*, which decides after lengthy consideration that it would prefer to be turned into a smart and immortal dragon. The carp's message is that everyone should shape his or her own life, and that people are responsible for their own happiness.

At the end of the street, the third or fourth Japanese Bridge spans a silt-choked tributary of the Thu Bon. Repeatedly washed away by floods or typhoons, the bridge we see today is a version from the mid-17th century. Over 800 buildings comprising traditional assembly halls, pagodas, warehouses, and residential blocks have been preserved, many of which can be visited. The entire historic city center was designated a UNESCO World Heritage Site in 1999, protecting these irreplaceable, generally still inhabited cultural monuments for the future but also attracting increasing numbers of tourists to the unique open-air museum that is Hoi An.

The inhabitants have accustomed themselves to the situation, and greet all visitors with Asian serenity. Even when faced with over-inquisitive tourists sticking their long noses into strangers' living quarters, the Vietnamese are a sociable people and seldom take it amiss. It's naturally better to wait at the door and pay the few dollars tour fee they request. In exchange, visitors receive a fascinating tour of a historic private house.

Westerners occasionally find it strange to inspect a house where people are still living, with children playing in the corner and grandparents waving from their armchairs. The Vietnamese are more relaxed about the situation, and are happy about tourists'

Young man, old man

Precisely 40 years after the first photo of the same place, Hoi An harbor. In terms of age, it could well be the same ferryman in both photographs. In 1967 the boy would have been around twelve, in 2007 the middle-aged man is around 52. Would the adult man perhaps recognize himself from the photo? We could not ask him. The buildings are certainly still in existence. The whole city was designated a UNESCO World Heritage Site in 1999 and is undergoing careful restoration.

1 Looking back at Hoi An in 1967, a city at war – What happened to the boy? **2** Looking to the future, Hoi An in 2007. This ferryman survived the war. **3** The Japanese Bridge from a fisherman's perspective. **4** Off the beaten (tourist) track – clay flutes fresh from the kiln. **5** Self-made success – a document laminator. **6** A test of courage – Monkey Bridge. **7** Craftsmanship as it was a century ago – shipbuilders at Hoi An.

ÉP DẺO
6
7

1 Creamy treats at Café Vienna. **2** A warm welcome at the reception desk. **3** Comfortable colonial style in the main house at Life Resort. **4** Poolside paradise – Hotel Hoi An Trails. **5** Room with pool view. **6** Chilling in the garden at Ha An.

interest in their way of life and about the change from their daily routine.

Quite another view can be found on the other side of the ancient harbor, easily accessible by crossing two bridges. From here, the Bach Dang river promenade is revealed in its full beauty. The glory of past centuries is easier to imagine from a distance. Its appearance must have survived almost unchanged through the ages; the houses directly on the waterfront have a particularly long history. And while we are here, we should continue our excursion on this side of Hoi An, where we can immerse ourselves in a different world of daily routine unaffected by tourism. Fishermen weave their nets, and in the shipbuilding yards workmen hammer enormous wooden nails into the timbers of the blue boats. The bamboo bridge to the ferry rocks gently in the evening breeze. And if we're lucky, a warm light streams across the river and thousands of twinkling reflections bob in its water: the Hoi An Lantern Festival. On the evening before full moon, Hoi An is illuminated by lanterns and candles in every window and in every store. The approaching

full moon must be welcomed appropriately and propitiated – and the best way to do this is with light, lots of light. Hundreds of little boats bearing candles float in the old harbor, people dance and play theater in the streets, the buildings flicker in the candlelight, and people sit outside doing what they enjoy most: eating together and talking.

The white beaches of Hoi An are only five kilometers (3 miles) away, at Cua Dai, and easily accessible by bicycle, moped or hotel shuttle bus. A boat trip from the harbor to the estuary is also worthwhile. And for a special experience, go to the last house before Cam Nam Bridge. The old woman who lives there rows her sampan to the sea and sings beautiful Vietnamese love songs.

Hoi An – 500 years of living history

What to see

The enchanted triangle of history at Hoi An lies between the fish market on the Thu Bon river, across the Tran Phu to the Japanese bridge, and back across Bach Dang to Cam Nam Bridge. Visitors will find many exquisite crafts from the daily life of this historic city; galleries, paintings, wood carvings, and gold and silver work range from tourist kitsch to Vietnamese art.

Where to stay

Life Resort Hoi An, 1 Pham Hong Thai St., Hoi An. Elegant hotel resort surrounded by palm groves in the heart of the Old Quarter, directly on the riverbank. Tel: 0084-51914555, e-mail: hoian@life-resorts.com, www.life-resorts.com

6

Hoi An Trails Resort, 276 Cua Dai Road, Hoi An. Between the beach and the city, secluded from the hustle and bustle but not far away: well-cared-for resort with comfortable rooms. Tel: 0084-51923999, e-mail: resa@hoiantrailsresort.com.vn, www.hoiantrailsresort.com.vn

Where to eat and drink

Ha An, 6–8 Phan Boi Chau St., has a beautiful terrace where local specialties from the Hoi An area can be enjoyed. The restaurant on the river bank at the *Life Resort* serves both high-class Vietnamese and international cuisine.

Special recommendations

Hire a moped and head for the white beaches at *Cua Dai* and the rural countryside surrounding Hoi An.
Photo-developing at *Truong Thanh*, 11 Le Loi, Hoi An. Excellent data and film processing services at fair prices in a tourist mecca. Tel: 0084-51910215, e-mail: quangminhlt@gmail.com

Information

Asia Explore, 87 Nghia Thuc St. Tel: 0084-82123133 or: 9242092, e-mail: asia-explore@vnn.vn, www.asia-explore.vn
Exotissimo Travel Vietnam Co Ltd, Saigon Finance Center 9 Dinh Tien Hoang, District 1, *Ho-Chi-Minh-City.* Tel: 0084-88251723-283, e-mail: go.vietnam@exotissimo.com, infoEXO@exotissimo.com, www.exotissimo.com

Along the Mandarin Road

The Pass of the Ocean Clouds and Hue

The Hai Van Pass, at an altitude of 500 meters (1,600 feet) between Da Nang and Hue, is not only the meteorological divide between North and South Vietnam, but also a mental divide between the very different temperaments in the two regions.

Fortunately, bad weather is forecast – a good omen for an interesting excursion into the mountains. The Pass of the Ocean Clouds, winding between Da Nang and Hue at an altitude of 500 meters (1,600 feet), should not be crossed in bright sunshine, which is, fortunately, infrequent. The altitude of the pass is frequently shrouded in cloud, and the gusty winds sweeping down from the 1,000-meter (3,400 feet) foothills of the Truong Son Mountains toss the gray masses around, heaping them into looming towers or pushing them across the asphalt like a fog bank before clearing the view over the bay of Da Nang in one direction and the peninsula of Lang Co in the other. A breathtaking, never-ending natural spectacle.

The long chain of mountains forms a lofty barrier that blocks the exchange of warm and cold air in the flat coastal regions, transforming Hai Van Pass into a vast weather cauldron, brewing up storms and rain between Vietnam's tropical south and subtropical north. A panoramic viewpoint from the topmost point enables visitors to marvel at the landscape stretching in both directions. The route leads past the ruined walls of wartime fortresses and bunkers and up some steps to the peak. Here, it becomes obvious why the pass held such strategic significance for many centuries. Two hundred years ago it was extended to form the first continuous route connecting Saigon and Hanoi. The section between Da Nang and Hue was named "the Road of the Mandarins" for its scenic beauty.

When we arrive in Hue the sky is cloudy – as so often. The dark walls, black citadel, imperial palaces, and tombs of Hue give the impression that this historical capital of Vietnam is plunged into state mourning.

Bonjour tristesse, bonjour Hue, melancholy city on the Perfume River, can you ever show a different face? The charming city nestling among hills and rice fields certainly can belie the heritage of its

1 Hai Van, the Pass of Ocean Clouds between Da Nang and Hue. **2** A popular subject for painters and photographers: the ao dai beauties of Hue. **3** Lang Co, peninsula at the Pass of Ocean Clouds. **4** Past and future are closely intertwined: morning gymnastics before the flagpole.

1 The imperial tomb of Tu Duc (1829–1883), a xenophobe now overrun by foreign tourists. **2** Thien Mu (17th century), the Pagoda of the Heavenly Woman, Hue's landmark. **3** Tomb of Emperor Minh Mang (1791–1841). **4** Imperial Palace. **5** Gate to the tomb of Emperor Minh Mang. **6** Holy water.

lugubrious Emperor Tu Duc. During his 36-year reign, longer than any other emperor, Hue's "sorrowful emperor" shaped the city's reputation with his doleful poems. Compounding the dolorous burden which the city bears is the constant presence of power

close at hand. For centuries, 13 emperors of the Nguyen dynasty ruled from the heart of Hue in a Chinese-style feudal court. The "citadel city" is bounded by eleven kilometers (5 miles) of walls. Walls conceal the former imperial city. Walls enclose the "Forbidden City" – walls which have perhaps immured the hearts of the people of Hue.

At the same time, Hue is traditionally a highly spiritual place of faith, where Vietnam's Buddhist heart beats strongest. It contains

around 300 temples and pagodas, the most important of which is Thien Mu Pagoda. 21 meters (69 feet) high, its seven storeys each represent the incarnation of one life of Buddha. It was here that the monk Thich Quang Duc took the decision to sacrifice his sole earthly life as a protest against the Catholic puppet government set in place by the Americans. On June 11, 1963, he got into a car and drove 900 kilometers (540 miles) to Saigon. Sitting in the lotus position at a crossroads, before the world's cameras, Thich Quang Duc was doused in petrol by nuns and monks and set himself on fire. His car, a small blue Austin, can be seen today in a glass case in the pagoda.

The landing stage for the dragon boats in front of the pagoda on the Perfume River is the starting point of an interesting tour. Only by viewing the city from the middle of the river can we gain a clear picture of its extent. As soon as we get back into a taxi, the clarity is gone. From tomb to tomb, from palace to temple, the drivers race through the narrow streets as if the monuments were about to disappear. There is no chance to develop a sense of direction. By

1 The guards at the mausoleum of King Khai Dinh, the last tomb of the Nguyen dynasty (1920–1931). **2** Memorial composed of china and glass mosaics. **3** Crypt. The mortal remains of the king lie 9 meters (30 feet) under the bronze statue. **4** Portrait of the king on the incense table.

the end of the journey we're guaranteed to have forgotten the century, the emperor, and the dynasty we've just encountered in our whirlwind passage.

It's time for a break, but there is no need to interrupt our journey through the history of the imperial city. Directly on the banks of the Perfume River lies La Résidence Hotel with terraces and gardens, affording wonderful views of the citadel and Trang Tien Bridge. The unusual building is a constituent part of Hue's more recent history. Built in 1930 as the official residence of the then Governor of Vietnam, its curved exterior façades with long horizontal lines and vertical ornamentation are characteristic of art deco architecture. The three adjacent buildings have a total of 122 rooms and suites, their old French charm and Asian opulence preserved to the present. Bao Dai, Vietnam's last emperor, and the still-officiating King Bhumipol of Thailand stayed here. The atmosphere in the hall and adjacent café recalls the colonial glory of the past. And yet the present warns: if we plan to occupy ourselves with the past, we have plenty ahead of us.

1 Lobby, bar and... **2** ... deluxe suite at "La Résidence." **3** Former governor's villa in a new light – Hotel La Residence. **4** Bathroom of the presidential suite. **5** Dreaming in a four-poster bed. **6** The hotel, salon of the arts, with touring exhibitions.

What about a mammoth tour of tombs and temples? Or perhaps a fragrant tour through the flower-laden air of the gardens and incense sticks smoking on the altars? Or simply a short city tour? Hue has so much to offer that it is advisable to consider a selection in advance. La Résidence is the place to go for good advice, and if we're lucky we'll find James Sullivan in the café. He knows Hue like the back of his hand and finds it a shame that most visitors seek nothing further than citadels, imperial tombs, and pagodas. Jim is American and a writer and journalist by profession, and has lived with his family in Hue for many years. Over a cozy cappuccino, he may first recommend a "stroll along Le Loi" – to kick-start visitors' addiction to this mysterious city.

The route takes us past the "raspberry-red railway station" to the Ho Chi Minh Museum and Quoc Hoc High School, which Ho

attended in his youth. We pass the People's Committee headquarters and come to Hotel Morin, a mighty building dating from 1901 which once again clearly demonstrates how Hue must have looked during the colonial era. The enormous hall is almost unchanged, and the salon de thé is a fine place to take tea or coffee in the afternoon and indulge in a little people-watching. However, if you happen to see Charlie Chaplin float around the corner with Paulette Goddard, pinch yourself; they spent their honeymoon here in 1939. In the evening, by way of respite, the city's other face beckons. Hello happiness, hello Hue, the friendly, cheerful city packed with artists, with its delightful market on the banks of the Perfume River, Vietnam's most exquisite cuisine and hosts of bright cafés – not a trace of melancholy. Dong Khoi, the boulevard between the cathedral and the riverbank, offers an inviting array of galleries and picturesque copyist studios for Old Masters. The "young masters" at their easels have no qualms about the source of their inspiration. After all, they say, they did actually paint the picture itself.

Pass of the Ocean Clouds and Hue

What to see
Pass of the Ocean Clouds on the way to Hue. The imperial palace and the imperial tombs of *Tu Duc*, *Khai Dinh*, *Minh Mang*.
Thien Mu Pagoda and the citadels are only a few of the many sights.
In the Imperial City of *Hue*, visitors are advised to find a knowledgeable guide, as otherwise it is easy to get lost and a tour becomes very tiring.

Where to stay
La Résidence Hotel & Spa, 5 Le Loi St., Hue. La Résidence was formerly the residence of the French governor of Hue. The building is practically in its original state, a jewel of colonial elegance. Tel: 0084-54837475,
e-mail: resa@la-residence-hue.com,
www.la-residence-hue.com
Pilgrimage Village, Boutique Resort 130 Minh Mang Road, Hue. Attractive hotel resort near the tombs. Tasteful single houses in an attractive garden setting. Tel: 0084-54885461, e-mail: info@pilgrimagevillage.com, www.pilgrimagevillage.com

6

Where to eat and drink
Mandarin Café, 24 Tran Cao Van St., Hue. Very cozy cafe serving typical Vietnamese specialties.
Tel: 0084-54821281, e-mail: mandarin@dng.vnn.vn

Special recommendations
Hue is a city of sensitive souls, probably the reason for its large population of artists; one example is the *Gallery of the Five Painters*.
Art Gallery Pho Co, 25 Huynh Thuc Khang-Tp. Hue. Contemporary art from Hue, highly recommended, beautiful works.
Tel: 0084-54527084
The impressive photo exhibition by Mr. Cu in the *Mandarin Café*. Now and again guests hold exhibitions – like *Doug* the American, alias Douglas Young.

Information
Tour information at *Hotel La Résidence*; special tips from James Sullivan, a US American in Hue. A journalist, he writes for *The New York Times*.
www.mandarinmedia.com

Dog days in Hue

It's raining in Hue. A permanent downpour for the last ten days. Slim fingers of water, mist, and drizzle penetrate every gap, every crack, every rucksack. The camera's electronic system begs "No, please, no" – an enforced break for film and chip. Photography is out of the question. "Not much to laugh about," complain the hotel's disappointed guests. Carmen Marienberg says, "No, definitely not, not in the next few days." But the manager of Hotel La Résidence has an idea. There is a café in the old quarter with a little photography exhibition. It belongs to Mr. Cu, a remarkably sensitive photographer of the country and its people. Perhaps he can help.

As an artist, Mr. Cu is thoroughly modest. Instead of discoursing on his beautiful pictures, he introduces Doug, his American friend. The reason: Doug Young is a US war vet who fought in Vietnam; his wife, Cindy, was a nurse at the field hospital. Now they have returned to the country which brought them together. Cindy teaches English at Hue University, while Doug and Cu document the beauty of the country in pictures. Cu says Doug taught him how to take photographs, and Doug says Cu taught him how to look. Together, driven by their common love of photography in Vietnam, they are a dream team. Some of Mr. Cu's photos are exhibited in the Mandarin Café. Doug's photos can be found on his website.

Mandarin Café, Hue City, Vietnam
Mr. Cu, the owner, Tel.: 054821281, e-mail: mandarin@dng.vnn.vn
Doug Young, Texas, USA blog: www.virtual-doug.com
Photos: www.pbase.com/doug_young

1 Ducks on parade, a favorite subject of Vietnamese photographer Cu. 2 Tableau with young ladies, a masterly picture by US veteran Doug Young. 3 The friends Cu and Doug.

Hanoi, Hanoi – a city that never sleeps. Midday break amid the bustle of the Old Quarter.

Austere Northern Beauty

Hanoi

Exploring a Dream City

Hanoi in the Company of Ms Vu Vietnam

Hanoi, almost a millennium of history on the banks of the Red River, is no city for dreamers – but a dream city for dynamic, positive people seeking to live their dreams.

Vietnam is like her country. On the small side, with a pleasing figure, slim-waisted, extremely friendly, extremely punctual, and full of drive, as the Hanoi people tend to be.

Ms Vu Vietnam is a tour and city guide, an art and culture maven for everything to do with her home city. Ms Frau Vietnam speaks enchanting German and naturally has everything immediately under control. "I went to school in the German Democratic Republic," she laughs. No beating about the bush here. And suddenly it's easy to understand why Hanoi is known as "Asia's Prussia."

As she is accustomed, Ms Vietnam immediately begins to forge strategic plans for fulfilling our production target: almost a millennium's worth of art, culture, exploration, and discovery. Her power, professionalism, and charm move into top gear – resistance is futile. Once again the white flag is raised before the victorious strategy of the Vietnamese. After the victory, peace negotiations are conducted in Café Mai near St. Joseph's Cathedral, over a *ca phe* – the strong Vietnamese coffee loaded with sweetened condensed milk.

It's a good start in the former French quarter before we begin our exciting journey through a city humming with prospects for the future – and occasionally tripped up by the past. The streets are still elegant with the grace of bygone days, but for much of this historic architecture it is only a matter of time before it is replaced by modern buildings. Will the "old lady," as Hanoi is affectionately known, lose her identity in this process of renewal? Will modern glass and steel edifices also destroy the unique charm of Hanoi's Eurasian culture? It is obvious that Hanoi's old city is in a disastrous state at precisely the points where it is also at its most beautiful. Generations of families have lived here, shaping the city's history over centuries. While life behind the dilapidated walls continues on its accustomed path, living conditions are deteriorating. Plans and action catalogs have been drawn up, directed at stopping the

1 A charming expert – city guide Ms Vu Vietnam. **2** Long Bien Bridge over the Red River. **3** Ho Chi Minh announces the Declaration of Independence – a picture in the History Museum. **4** The Turtle Pagoda in Hoan Kiem Lake.

1 Bamboo or what? – a whole lane dedicated to the tall shoots. **2** Not a one-way street – "Coffin Alley" in Hanoi's artisan quarter. **3** Braking baby – bamboo playpens. **4** Immortalized in stone – grave headstones. **5** Lanterns and crackers, the colorful specialties of Paper Alley.

decay. Bringing light and air into the city by introducing gaps between the buildings is an idea aimed at improving the living conditions of rear-courtyard dwellers. However, this involves targeted demolition and the skilled, painstaking construction of new buildings behind ancient façades, themselves crumbling at an increasing pace. It's almost as if Sisyphus and the devil had signed a pact to enclose Hanoi's Old Quarter in their power.

Not even the rigorously progressive wing of Hanoi's city planners are rejoicing. They are well aware that every act of demolition is ultimately doing far more harm than good, because Hanoi natives love their city more passionately than is customary among Vietnamese. They are sympathetic to the condition of the Old Quarter, as they would be to an elderly lady appearing at the ball in the same dress for the twentieth time – but as soon as the first chords

5

of the opening waltz ring out, they push their dark thoughts aside and succumb to the city's bewitching fascination.

Daily performances on the open stage – Hanoi's Old Quarter – are similar. City planning concerns are swept away on a tide of colors, scents, and sounds. The Old Quarter plays a key role in a kind of live Vietnamese folk theater, more authentic than anywhere else in Vietnam. The stage comprises 36 lanes and alleyways, and the set and props are made up of fresh flowers, lanterns, baguettes, coffins, bamboo, and open-air food stalls. The actors wear their own clothes and play themselves. The audience is part of the scenery, the production is guided by intuition alone, and the director is everyday life itself. Scenes are unrehearsed and never repeated. Take "Coffin Alley," for example. We see a man lashing a child's coffin onto the pillion of his motorbike with an elastic band, unable to complete his task immediately because of his shaking hands. Once his burden is firmly fixed, he threads his way into the stream of mopeds flowing by, and the black coffin flashes once or twice in the hard morning sun – a final affirmation of life.

Scene two. More lanes lined with needful things of daily life are waiting to be explored. Next to the open-air barber, tires are changed, chickens' rumps plucked, and ears cleaned out with cotton buds by the searching light of a torch. In Paper Alley, bags are glued together and lanterns folded. Money is cheap here, too, stacked in neat bundles. It's dollars, of course; dong, the Vietnamese currency, is unworthy of being burnt on the altar as a gift to the ancestors. Dollars, still the cool symbol of wealth, burn more efficiently. The friendly flower girls from the adjacent stand are prettier than the flowers – but Ms Vietnam imposes the stern hand of discipline – and anyway, it's time for lunch.

From noon onward, the intoxicating scent of Hanoi's food stalls settles over the city and paralyses its life. The very thought of *pho* acts like a hypnotic elixir on the Vietnamese. Once the scent lies in their nostrils, there's no holding them back. *Pho ga* or *pho bo*, noodle soup with chicken or beef with celery and spring onion, is the most delicious temptation in the history of noodle soup. Add a dollop of friendly, welcoming atmosphere: simple, practical, vibrant.

1 The rear of the Old Quarter gate in Hanoi. **2** Got a beef? – 150 kilos of steak on the hoof atop this moped. **3** Seniors on the road under their own steam. **4** Trains on Long Bien Bridge. **5** Cyclo café in the Old Quarter – rickshaw drivers take a rest. **6** A novel pillion. **7** A beastly heavy load. **8** Washing whiter – view from Long Bien Bridge.

Knee-high plastic stools compel taller diners to adopt a straight-backed posture, while concerned co-slurpers warn smilingly of the hot lime and chili pickle. *Nuoc mam* fish sauce does the rounds. It's a truly uplifting experience to be welcomed so warmly into this small world of the diner. Ms Vietnam is proud of her guests, and they're proud of Vietnam.

The next suggestion on our program is as appropriate as if we had just passed an examination in Vietnamese lifestyle. After eating, we're ready for a rickshaw and willing to let ourselves be transported on this wheeled sofa. It isn't to everyone's taste; some are worried at the principle of being carried through the city by person-power, while some are simply scared to death. Also known as cyclos, these vehicles offer an extremely unfamiliar perspective for European passengers; when lounging, they face the exhaust pipes of mopeds passing at knee level and their view is flanked by the

8

wings of the cars on each side. But when facing forward, they have an excellent view by looking over the shoulder of the frantically pedalling driver. A friendly driver will occasionally turn round to his passengers, steering with one hand to explain the sights more clearly. Of course, the result is a larger tip, which adds a wonderful dynamism to the cyclo ride.

Fortunately, we locate the hand-grips fairly fast, and our search for them is an excellent distraction from the red traffic lights our driver is blithely ignoring – a habit of his, and probably an improvement on the continuous emergency stops he would otherwise need. We're not alone in our situation; when we are finally able to open our eyes, we notice that the entire stream of mopeds, cars, and cyclos is progressing fluidly. Yet the days of cycle rickshaws in the city are numbered, and more and more signs prohibiting them are appearing in the streets. But if they are completely forbidden, however, will people be able to transport mattresses, cupboards, whole pigs, heavy statues of Buddha, and five-person families cheaply through Hanoi ?

Our adventurous tour of the city ends at the great square before Hanoi's attractive opera house. Mr Van Thoung plunges back into the endless stream of cyclos without the slightest sign of tiredness. His newly alighted passengers note that the sidewalk in front of the opera feels soft and strangely spongy. Ms Vietnam offers two good suggestions, the first of which is received with enthusiasm after the cyclo ride: a snack at the chocolate buffet of Hanoi's most beautiful hotel. The second idea, of watching the bridal couples at the opera house, will have to wait.

This is the way Hanoi should stay until the end of time, we think as we gaze up at the elegant façade of Hanoi's Hotel Sofitel Metropole. Built in 1901 in French colonial style, the hotel is a monument to the successful preservation of the historic past for the benefit of the future. It is both a classic landmark in Hanoi's center and an ultra-traditional, luxury, five-star hotel, said to have impressed Somerset Maugham and Graham Greene as well as Jane Fonda, Roger Moore, Joan Baez, and Michael Caine – and when we enter through the revolving door and see the interior, we are convinced. This is a new, stunningly vibrant take on the elegant French culture of an entire era.

In this interior of mahogany and marble, elegant drapes and stucco, time seems to have stood still. An intoxicating scent wafts through

1 Balancing on one leg – Chua Mot Cot Pagoda in Hanoi. 2 As important as the bride's dress – family portrait in front of the elegant opera house. 3 Retirees at Hoan Kiem Lake. 4 Collective fitness – school sports class in front of St. Joseph's Cathedral.

the hall. In front of Le Club bar stands a chocolate buffet laden with the most delicious pâtisserie we have ever set eyes on. At least, that could be the feeling of anyone unable to fully appreciate the somewhat idiosyncratic flavor of the brightly colored, heavy, sweet cakes available from Vietnamese bakers. These alluring creations sparkle like jewels on the buffet in the unique atmosphere. It's going to be a perfect afternoon.

The French colonial rulers must once have felt the same as we do now at the chocolate buffet; the pleasures of the palate could not satisfy them for long – after all, they had planned a lengthy stay. Far from their own land, they were homesick for other highlights of

4

their national culture, and called for centers of music, dance, and opera to be founded. Hanoi's opera house was built in 1911 and named "la petite cousine" by the French – the "little cousin" of the Opéra Garnier in Paris, housing performances of the French romantics in an atmosphere of colonial cultivation. Thus did the French soothe their homesickness, by transforming Hanoi into the most nearly French city in all Indochina.

Until September 17, 2006, no operas had been staged in Hanoi for fifty-two years, since the end of French rule in 1954. The revival saw an Austrian-Vietnamese co-production of Mozart's *Magic Flute*, played by the Hanoi Philharmonic Orchestra, conducted by Wolfgang Gröhs, and directed by Manfred Waba. The artists, singing in German, came from the Hanoi Conservatory of Music. The historic event at the Hanoi Opera was received with unbounded enthusiasm.

Each day on the round steps in front of the opera house, a performance of a different kind takes place. It features two main characters, hundreds of extras, and an unknown number of photographers and film directors.

In the cooler months from October to March, the Vietnamese go crazy for weddings. After all, who wants to marry in temperatures of 40 °C (104 °F) and maximum humidity? And since the lunar calendar must also be considered when fixing the happy day, only a few specific dates are possible. As a result, quite a line builds up in front of the opera house, and anyone planning to take photographs of the building without a garnish of bridal veils should buy a postcard, or be prepared to get up at the crack of dawn.

The easiest way is to stay nearby at the Hilton Hanoi Opera. Many of the rooms overlook the opera house, and the soft side-lighting after sunrise adds a glorious brilliance to photographs. An early dip

1 Hanoi's most elegant hotel is the Sofitel Metropole. **2** Naughty but nice – the chocolate buffet at the Metropole. **3** Afternoon champagne: the terrace at the Hilton Hotel Opera. **4** An oasis of calm in the city: room at the Sofitel Metropole. **5** Literature and international books at Bookworm Hoang Van Truong.

in the big open-air pool kick-starts the circulation. The enormous foyer is filled with a pleasant mixture of businesspeople and tourists. The cosmopolitan flair of a rising metropolis is highly infectious – the air is perfumed with the scent of the future. All the traditional aspects that comprise the charm of the Vietnamese have been retained, particularly their hospitality and their delicious food; in fact, specialties from the north are particularly delicious, as head chef Pham Xuan Cuong demonstrates by serving a simple North Vietnamese dish from his state-of-the-art kitchen in the glamorous Ba Mien restaurant overlooking Hanoi's old opera house.

Despite – or perhaps because of – this mixture of traditional commitment and contemporary zeitgeist, Hanoi gives no cause for worry. Of course the "old lady" is understandably unwilling to celebrate the next twenty years of opera balls in the same old dress; but even after donning her new outfit, she plans to retain her personality. She and her people are far too aware of their traditions. No one finds life here burdensome. Of course, there is

plenty that could be different, and naturally better – which provides fuel for discussions day in, day out. But when the next day dawns, Hanoi's inhabitants are happy that much has stayed just the way it is.

Ms Vietnam sits in a plump armchair in the enormous foyer, somewhat lost in its bulk. She proudly produces her list with only one item still to tick off. In the city of thirty lakes, Hoan Kiem Lake occupies a special place in the hearts of the Hanoians, a historic and mystic location and a meeting point for lovers and leisure-seekers.

In the heart of Hanoi between the Old Quarter and the great east-west connecting roads, it lies like an oasis of peace in the bustling city. In the morning it is a meeting point for tai chi exercisers, with joggers flying past. In the evening, the pensioners line up on the park benches, just as their counterparts do in New York or San Francisco, London or Sydney. Sometimes they hold hands, an uncommon sight in Vietnam. But here at the lake a different set of rules applies; after all, it is regarded as the most romantic place in the city. The golden turtle god that lives in the lake guards the magic sword of Emperor Le Loi, which he used to drive the Chinese from the country and was forced to return after his victory.

Hanoi – austere northern beauty

How to get there
Regular flights from Washington and New York via Tokyo with *Vietnam Airlines*, from London via Frankfurt or Paris with *Lufthansa* and *Vietnam Airlines.*

What to see
The 36 artisans' lanes and the whole of the Old Quarter. No special recommendations can be made; Hanoi is a city that everyone must explore for themselves.

Where to stay
Sofitel Metropole Hanoi, 15 Ngô Quyên St., Hanoi. World-class hotel combining the height of Vietnamese and European elegance.
Tel: 0084-48266919, e-mail: sofitelhanoi@hn.vnn.vn, www.sofitel.com

5

Hilton Hanoi Opera Hotel, 1 Le Thanh Tong St., Hanoi. World-class hotel with international business atmosphere.
Tel: 0084-49330500, e-mail: frontofficeadmin.hanoi@hilton.com, www.hanoi.hilton.com
Thien Thai Hotel, Sky-Garden Club, 45 Nguyen Truong To St., Hanoi. Friendly budget hotel in the Old Quarter.
Tel: 0084-47164126

Where to eat and drink
Le Tonkin, Vietnamese restaurant, 14 Ngo Van So, Hanoi. Cozy luxury restaurant, superb cuisine. Tel: 0084-49433457
Highway4 Restaurant, 18 Yen Phu St., Hanoi. Typical Vietnamese restaurant extending over three floors. Tel: 0084-47150577, e-mail: info@highway4.com, www.highway4.com

Special recommendations
Hanoi Press Club, 59 A Ly Thai To St., Hanoi. International meeting place. Tel: 0084-49340888, e-mail: vietai@hanoi-pressclub.com, www.hanoi-pressclub.com
Bookworm Hoang Van Truong, 15a Ngo Van So, Hanoi. International press and books. Tel: 0084-49437226, e-mail: bookworm@fpt

Information
Exotissimo Travel, Main Office, 26 Tran Nhat Duat St.
Tel: 0084-48282150, e-mail: infoEXO@exotissimo.com, go.vietnam@exotissimo.com, www.exotissimo.com

1
2
3
4

Visiting "Uncle Ho"

Hanoi – Mausoleum and a Thousand-year-old Culture

"Nothing is more valuable than independence and freedom." So said Ho Chi Minh – whose name means "enlightened will" – speaking at Ba Dinh Square in Hanoi in 1945, in allusion to the first lines of the American Declaration of Independence. Since 1975 the same words have been displayed on the wall of the Ho Chi Minh Mausoleum at the same site.

Today, Ms Vietnam is different. A little nervous, slightly worried, somewhat reserved, over-punctual, and bubbling over with explanations. All this because she is embarrassed to address her guests about rules of behavior for a visit to the nation's holiest shrine. It's torment to her sensitive, tolerant, Vietnamese soul to inform visitors that shorts may under no circumstances be worn to enter the mausoleum of the honorable freedom fighter and founder of the state, Ho Chi Minh. At the sarcophagus itself, speaking, photographing, stopping or leaving the line are all prohibited.

As she speaks, we automatically check the length of our pants, fiddle with our top shirt buttons, switch off our cameras.

The atmosphere in the long, dead-straight line before the plain cashier's office has something of the nostalgic Socialist charm of a former border control point between West Germany and East Berlin. Fortunately, all of that is long past and almost forgotten – but the gigantic white tomb of Ho Chi Minh can't be wiped out so easily; it's definitely built to last for eternity. And the original architectural plans based on Lenin's tomb are actually supposed to resemble the outlines of a lotus flower; however, the monolithic style of the mausoleum's Soviet builders has crushed any immediate resemblance.

While the line of international visitors slowly shuffles forward, Ms Vietnam takes advantage of the brief inattention of the white-clad soldiers to convey a few whispered facts. Ho Chi Minh died of heart failure on September 2, 1969 at the age of 79. But because that was Vietnamese Independence Day, the "official" date of death was moved to September 3, enabling both events to be commemorated separately. The victory over the French at Dien Bien Phu in 1954 was his greatest triumph, and guaranteed

1 Vietnam's stronger sex – a place of honor in the Women's Museum. **2** The country's history in the History Museum. **3** Mr Hung receives his guests at the restaurant Le Tonkin. **4** Visiting "Uncle Ho"– Ho Chi Minh's mausoleum.

1 Ho Chi Minh's last living quarters and command center. **2** "Uncle Ho's" office. **3** The Battle of Bach Dang, History Museum. **4** Mother Vietnam – the future rests on her shoulders. **5** Hoa Lo Prison; US prisoners of war called it the "Hanoi Hilton." **6** Ho Chi Minh's conference room.

his immortality for the people of Vietnam; so what's a day here or there?

Although Ho Chi Minh did not live to see military victory over the Americans, the moral victory in the Tet Offensive in 1968 was, in a way, a continuation of his victory at Dien Bien Phu. It was only a matter of time before this terrible disaster would be repeated by the Americans.

Only a few minutes to go before we can walk past the embalmed body of President Ho Chi Minh, founder of the state, revolutionary, and victor over France and the USA, lying in state in a glass coffin. But no more than ten absolutely silent seconds elapse before we are shoved, waved, and ordered onward. And yet it is a strange experience to have seen the body of such a charismatic man.

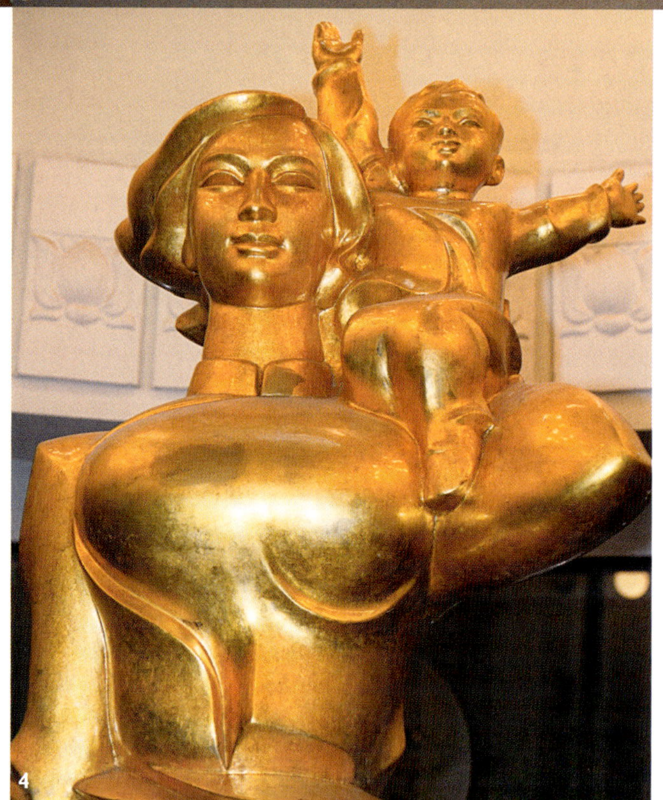

In the past, the mortal remains of Uncle Ho undertook an annual journey to his Socialist brothers in Moscow for cosmetic retouching treatment. He is now spared this stressful experience, as reembalming measures are performed at home in Hanoi. Perhaps these, too, will cease in the future. Ho Chi Minh, who requested that his remains should be cremated but never embalmed, had also specified his final journey in his will. However, as yet, the Politburo has refused to grant their leader's last wish – their national icon is still essential.

Perhaps when general understanding arises that Uncle Ho did a good job, but that the wounds of time can only be healed by the balm of a new national confidence instead of by embalming old ideologies at all costs, "at the expense of thinking further," perhaps then Ho Chi Minh can begin his final journey, and his final wish for his ashes to be scattered equally throughout North and South Vietnam will be fulfilled. May his wish come true, this people's hero and worldwide symbol of peace for a whole generation, born in a humble village in Central Vietnam.

Changing of the guard at the mausoleum – no bearskins, but white uniforms and military precision. A twelve-voice women's choir falls into reverent silence. Tourists automatically straighten their non-existent ties, cameras are forgotten. The ceremony is greeted with awed attention. Thick white lines on Ba Dinh Square have already roughly sorted the many spectators; now the soldiers complete the fine-tuning with brief, severe glances. Now we understand why Ms Vietnam was so unlike herself this morning.

We finally relax in the park in front of the president's palace. The little lake, the house next to the garage where Uncle Ho's car still stands, and the simple house on piles give an impression of how he must have spent his last years in Hanoi, where he had achieved his life's goal, the freedom and thus the independence of his people.

On August 24, 1945, the last emperor of the Nguyen dynasty, Bao Dai, handed his insignia of rule and his certificate of abdication to the representatives of the Communist government – the end of a 150-year dynasty.

On September 2, 1945, Ho Chi Minh read the Declaration of

1 Wild Lotus, Hanoi's top restaurant. **2** The service team at Le Tonkin. **3** Vietnamese gourmet cuisine, French-style, at the Wild Lotus. **4** Doorway to heaven: the entrance to Wild Lotus. **5** History Museum.

Independence on Ba Dinh Square in front of half a million people. Today, in the adjacent Ho Chi Minh Museum, the recording of Uncle Ho's speech can still be heard – the voice of a man who shaped world history, but who is commemorated as "Uncle" in the history books. The reason for this is that in Vietnamese family clans it is not the father, but the father's eldest brother, known as bac, who commands the most respect. The form of address "Uncle Ho" is therefore a sign of the highest respect.

Hanoi's most attractive museum is close to Song Hong, the Red River. Today, the former governor's residence of the French regents houses the National History Museum, presenting tasteful exhibitions of Vietnam's rich history in a factual, informative style. The Declaration of Independence is naturally featured, in the form of a large-format, brilliantly colored panorama painting in naïve style. Not far away is an equally enormous panorama of the battle at

Bach Dang River, where the legendary army commander Ngo Quyen made a successful bid to free the country from a thousand years of Chinese rule. Ngo Quyen used a brilliant trick to lure the enemy's heavy junks into the Bach Dang estuary, where he had set iron-tipped wooden stakes in the mud; as the tide receded, the Chinese fleet was impaled on the stakes. Ngo Quyen was the first king of independent Vietnam. A comparison to the battle between David against Goliath is no coincidence.

It is also not by chance that Ms Vietnam, our specialist for art and culture, now urges us to move on – to the Women's Museum. The place of honor occupied by this museum in the center of Hanoi is echoed by the status of women in Vietnam's history and present-day society. "Mother Vietnam" is the symbol of family cohesion, a characteristic most highly venerated by the Vietnamese. "Vietnamese women weave the world together" is written at the entrance, together with "When the enemy attacks the home, women must fight." Ms Vietnam is visibly pleased at the fascination the museum exerts on her guests.

Hanoi – mausoleum and a thousand years of art

What to see
The *Ho Chi Minh Mausoleum*; *Uncle Ho*'s house with his offices, in their original state.
The *Women's Museum*, the *Literature Temple*, the *One-Pillar Pagoda*, the *Ethnology* and *History Museums*, the *Hanoi Hilton* – not the hotel, but the former prison for US pilots taken prisoner in the war.

5

Where to stay
See recommendations on page 137.

Where to eat and drink
Wild Lotus Restaurant and Lounge, 55A Nguyen Du, Hanoi. Gourmet restaurant for the wealthy.
Tel: 0084-49439342

Special recommendations
Co Do Gallery, 46 Hang Bong, Hanoi. The best galleries for the classic Vietnamese art of lacquer painting can be found in the Old Quarter and near the *Hilton Hotel*.
www.codogallery.com

Information
Exotissimo Travel, Main Office, 26 Tran Nhat Duat St., Hanoi.
Tel: 00844 828 2150,
e-mail: infoEXO@exotissimo.com,
go.vietnam@exotissimo.com,
www.exotissimo.com

A Thousand Pots and a Man of Mystery

Bat Trang – Rice Bowls for Millions

Rice, vegetables, herbs – the three pillars of Vietnamese cuisine – have a heavy duty. 85 million hungry bellies to be filled every day. This basic diet is supplemented by many an additional delicacy – but where do all the rice bowls come from?

The road to Bat Trang leads across the Red River by Chuong Cuong Bridge and into the district of Gia Lam – Hanoi's first outlying district to the east, on the other side of the Song Hong. But we're not going there yet, says Vietnam, now on first-name terms without the "Ms" – even though the professional guide in her would like to refuse, she looks down in slight embarrassment, but accepts smiling. "Good morning, Vietnam, what's on the program today?" The market, the bridge, the ceramic village and the specialty restaurant!

The market next to Long Bien Bridge is an encounter between past and future offering more striking contrasts than anywhere else in Hanoi's teeming metropolis. A masterpiece of ugliness, the bridge was designed and built by Monsieur Eiffel a good century ago and appropriately celebrated as the fast lane into the age of technology, ensuring that goods transported to the city of Hanoi from the surrounding countryside arrived faster, fresher and more profitably.

But the grim-looking bridge did not transform the traditional lives of the rural population as quickly as originally announced. As always throughout Vietnam's history, new influences are interwoven with old values only slowly. The market, next to the bridge, represents the tenacious survival of a microcosm that operates to its own laws. It's well worth embarking on your own voyage of discovery – all you need is to be willing to open up to the people and greet them with curiosity, and you'll step into a world full of anecdotes from a traditional facet of Vietnam that will hopefully survive long into the future.

Bat means bowl, and trang is a workshop. The name Bat Trang suddenly becomes crystal clear: bowl workshop. But in Bat Trang, the center of earthenware and ceramics on the eastern bank of the Red River, nothing can yet be seen of the 85 million rice bowls that, in theory, the Vietnamese people require every day. But the little streets are already abuzz in the morning light. Horse-drawn

1 Turning on the skill – hand-crafted rice bowls. **2** Reading the newspaper while waiting for custom. **3** Beware: fragile dog – ceramic art at the market. **4** Vase in a haystack – bicycle serving as a truck.

1
2
3
4
5
6
7
8
9

carts piled high with packing straw for the potters trot up to the packing ramps at a leisurely pace. Mopeds overloaded with ceramic pots groan under their burden, which must weigh twice as much as rider and vehicle combined. Old brick kilns cough acrid smoke into the morning air. This is a proven combination of tradition and technology, with a history dating back to the 14th century and still the direct or indirect means of support for most of the village's 3,000 inhabitants.

High-pitched giggling peals from a workshop, awakening our curiosity and also helping to solve the great mystery of Bat Trang. Inside, a long table stands full of rice-bowls as far as the eye can see, and around 20 girls are painting simple but attractive patterns on them with nimble fingers. It's a fast process, at least one bowl per minute per girl and 20 girls, 60 minutes in an hour – when does it all add up to 85 million?

Close by on the way back to Hanoi, a little path snakes up to a mysterious house. Than Dao, a man with mystical appearance and penetrating stare, invites the guests into his living room, considering for a long time before speaking a few words. Photos of the complete process of preparing a snake? He takes a powerful pull on his dieu cay, the mouthpiece of his water-pipe, and discusses the matter with his sons Huy, Truong and Thiet. Their conclusion is that the current lunar constellation will prevent any bad luck from being created by the photos. Only the pictures of killing the snake would be a problem, as three people should never be in the same photo at once.

Mr Dao finally explains the ritual and the "courses". The snake's heart and gall-bladder are cut out, the gall and blood mixed with alcohol and drunk immediately, after which the heart is eaten. This is claimed to mobilize enormous energy, encouraging potency and strengthening the body's defenses. As for dosage, the more poisonous the snake, the more powerful the effect. The menu begins with fried cobra with broccoli and water-spinach; the chef's special recommendation for dessert is snake in plum juice with lotus seeds. Between these delicacies, snake soup with grated bones and spring rolls with cobra filling are served.

1 Mystical snake-charming. **2** Catching the cobra. **3** The fatal stab. **4** Extracting the gall bladder and blood. **5** A powerful mix – snake juices and alcohol. **6** For potency and health. **7** Vietnamese Viagra? **8** Snake ragout. **9** The cook. **10** Cobra with chopsticks. **11** Food testers Phuong, Hien and Tuan.

Bat Trang – rice bowls for millions

What to see
The *potters' village Bat Trang* with its ceramics and potteries is world famous, with products exported to France and Japan. The brick kilns are no younger than the last century – and have never been cold since they were built.

Where to stay
Day excursion from Hanoi. For recommendations see page 137.

Where to eat and drink
Snake specialties at *Thanh Dao*, Viet Hung, Le Mat.

Not to everyone's taste – but this applies only to the menu; the restaurant itself is attractive and elegant.
Visitors unwilling to try the snake dishes can wriggle out of it. The others will make a very special and tasty experience.
Tel: 0084-48274295.

Special recommendation
On the return journey to Hanoi, take a detour through *Hai Ba Trung* district on the Red River. Here the lanes are too narrow for cars. The market is small and very traditional; tourists are rarely seen here.

Junks that moor here must leave the bay before sunrise.

Nothing But Nature

Fascination of the Northern Coast

1
2
3
4

What Did the Dragon Throw?

Halong Bay and its Legends

*Some say rocks, some say pearls.
How exactly was Halong Bay created by Mother Dragon
while she was protecting her children, the Viets,
from the Chinese army?*

The official report goes like this: Halong Bay in northeast Vietnam was created 30 to 50 million years ago when the Asian seabed began to rise. Deposits of coral from the depths of the ocean were pushed to the surface, solidifying in the sun and air into the typical cone-shaped hills of this bizarre, mysterious landscape strewn with over 2,000 rocky crags and limestone islets, numerous stalactite caves, and equally numerous legends.

Unofficially, so the story goes, Ha Long, the "descending dragon," was sent by the gods to bring order to the east coast. The Chinese were again hungry to acquire the Viets' fertile country and planned to invade it with their huge navy. At this, Mother Dragon became so angry that she strode from the far north across the Tonkinese Alps, thrashing her long tail and destroying all the cliffs in the area. As the tumbling rocks destroyed the great ships, she drove the remainder of the fleet to flight by breathing fire.

Since those times, Halong Bay has been lined with lofty cliffs and crags like watchtowers, and no ship can now sneak in undetected. There is a milder version, however. Instead of flying into a rage, Mother Dragon is said to have scattered a handful of pearls over the bay, which were transformed into the 2,000 crags and islets that make the bay one of the most beautiful places on earth. Many Vietnamese prefer the peaceful, poetic version of the origins of a paradise which is by no means free from danger. Although the Chinese fleet is no longer an imminent hazard, the bay is lashed several times a year by typhoons roaring in from the South China Sea and causing considerable damage. It's the signal for the 300 fishing families that have lived for centuries in their floating houses in the middle of the bay to seek out the caves and grottoes on the islets, which offer effective protection and security and often shield them better than hiding-places on the nearby coast.

Since Halong Bay was designated a UNESCO World Natural Heritage Site, environmental protection plans have prohibited further

1 Fresh-caught in Halong Bay – lunch on the upper deck. **2** Tung, the captain of the junk, prefers engine power. **3** No camera, no good – a Japanese family tours the caves. **4** As safe as it gets – crossing the bay under the protection of dragons.

1 Sailing into the underworld – venturing into the largest cave at the bay. **2** Sun again at last – light at the end of the cave. **3** "Uncle Ho" was here – viewing point and entrance to Hanq Dau Go grotto. **4** By kayak through the bay – an excursion from the paddle steamer *Emeraude*. **5** Subterranean enchantment as colorful lighting illuminates stalagmites in blue and pink.

families from settling in the bay. However, these regulations are almost futile as the bay's UNESCO status attracts increasing numbers of visitors, who represent further environmental risks. Over the long term, the bay's popularity may have a more serious impact on the environment than the regular annual typhoons.

Yet the first signs of enlightenment are already in evidence, together with active environmental protection measures. The number of junks and boats will not be increased, and a new harbor will be constructed to handle thousands of passengers from all over the world more efficiently. A further hope is that waste disposal problems on the junks will be treated with more environmental responsibility than has hitherto been the case – and initial progress has already been made.

Sailors, staff, and passengers on the junks have definitely begun to exercise more care in disposing of plastic bags of garbage, and certainly have nothing to do with the bluish oil patches shimmering on the surface of the emerald water.

Halong Bay lies on a major shipping route, and is also the site of large-scale industrial plants, where coal mines produce endless quantities of waste water and dirt. Since UNESCO threatened to withdraw the title of World Natural Heritage Site from the Vietnamese, ships are being rerouted and sewage and waste disposal plants constructed. This could be seen as the modern version of the "descending dragon," today called UNESCO, which has rapped the Vietnamese firmly on the knuckles.

The journey from Hanoi to Ha Long is about a three-hour drive. The scenery is uneventful. After our early start in Hanoi, a snooze until we reach the junk harbor of Ha Long seems like an excellent

plan. The scene is not as romantic as the name "junk" might suggest. This severe concrete building could be in any Western port, and when we are called upon to pay a large sum of "toilet dong," we realize that tourism is the ruling principle. Let's get out of here! But how do we find "our" junk? A bobbing sea of masts gives not the slightest clue. The wooden boats are moored in ranks of four, and a Babylonian hubbub of languages stifles our attempt to deliver the carefully rehearsed question, "Where is my junk?" Our bags are already on board – but where?

The climax of our attempts to board is still to come. A narrow gangplank leads from the pier to the junk, from railing to railing. We're tempted to hand over all our valuables voluntarily before stepping onto the frail plank, convinced that we will never make it to the other side without a submersion.

But junks favor the brave, and brisk Vietnamese hands reach out to grasp us, so that before we know what's happening we have safely crossed the treacherously swaying plank over the muddy harbor waters. The sight of our delightful cabin on the *Bai Tho Dschunke* makes us forget all the torment, and our bags are sitting next to the cozy bunks – transported as if by magic. All that worry for nothing!

It's fascinating to observe the scene as we sail out of Ha Long harbor. The British are drinking brandy and betting that the junks will sink each other. The French are opening champagne and crying, "Mon dieu!" Germans are swigging ice-cold "Ha Noi" beer and devising a more efficient course for the captain.

His name is Tung, and he takes it all in good part. Captain Tung has steered his boat through the bay for many years – by engine power: the sails are only set for effect to please the passengers. It's obvious that he loves his job at the helm. Captain Tung is happy to explain the legends attached to the rocks and crags, weaving between turtle-headed sea monsters, dodging dragons, and skilfully evading a pouncing tiger.

Smiling, he points into the blue sky, proudly telling us, "Look, an

1 Dragon's-eye view – from the crow's nest of the junk. **2** Not kitsch, but nature pure and simple: junks moored for the night. **3** The *Bai-Tho* team – waiter Nga, chef Tuyen, and waitress Truong. **4** Cabin on the *Bai Tho*. **5** Restaurant deck of the *Indochina Sails* junk. **6** Luxury cabin on the *Indochina Sails* junk. **7** Cabin on the *Indochina Sails* junk.

eagle!" Nowhere can more species of animal be found than around Halong Bay.

At sunset Captain Tung steers into a beautiful bay – albeit not voluntarily; all junks must anchor at this location as part of the strict environmental regulations. Yet it is fascinating to see the illuminated junks gathered at sunset in a fairy-tale scene. And when the sun has fully set, the cooks in the tiny galleys also prove they can work magic, with seafood straight from Halong Bay served in the wood-paneled restaurant on the upper deck. Just one of the highlights of a junk cruise in mystery-enshrouded Halong Bay.

At sunrise the paddle-steamer *Emeraude* awaits its passengers. It's a ship which, at first glance, appears to be as much a part of

5

6

7

I Sundeck on the paddle steamer *Emeraude*. 2 Back to the mother ship – the kayaks are coming. 3 The stories the *Emeraudes* could tell – the colonial-era paddle steamers. 4 Luxury cabin on the main deck. 5 Bonjour in the bathroom. 6 Walkie-talkies and speedboat – the photo assistants of *Indochina Sails*.

Halong Bay as champagne and caviar is a part of the fishermen's table. But the *Emeraude* is actually a traditional ship from the French colonial era.

Three brothers from the south of France had made their fortunes by trading foodstuffs and opium in Indochina and established a small fleet in Halong Bay. The ships were named *Emeraude*, *Rubin*, *Perle*, and *Saphir*, and were truly the jewels of that era's tourism. The *Emeraude* sank off Hai Phong in 1937; the other ships did not survive the end of the colonial era. In 1999 the new *Emeraude* was recreated at Hai Phong shipyards from an old postcard, and began its new and successful life as an exclusive cruise ship in Halong Bay in 2002.

Halong Bay – packed with legends

What to see
Hang Dau Go grotto, with the most beautiful panoramic view of the bay. Visit the floating villages.

Where to stay
Accommodation on junks or paddle steamer *Emeraude*. Cabins and berths of all standards and prices from standard to comfort, some even luxury class.

Where to eat and drink
The onboard restaurants offer a cozy atmosphere with views of the bay gliding past. Magnificent seafood from the bay, fresh vegetables, fine wines.

Special recommendations
90-step climb to *Hang Dau Go grotto* with enormous caves. Kayak tour to the floating villages from the paddle steamer. Take a photo tour in dinghies at sunset!

Information
Always choose an experienced and reputable travel partner:
Bai Tho Tourist Ltd.Co., 175 Cao Xanh, *Halong City*. Tel: 0084-33826274, Office *Hanoi* Kim Tours & Travel: 62 Hang Bo Str., Tel: 0084-49124340, e-mail: info@baithojunk.com, www.baithojunk.com
Emeraude Classic Cruises, Mr. Kurt Walter, c/o Press Club, 59A Ly Thai To Street, *Hanoi*. Tel: 0084-49340888, Hotline: 0084-913028100, e-mail: sales@emeraude-cruises.com, www.emeraude-cruises.com
Exotissimo Travel, Main Office, 26 Tran Nhat Duat St., *Hanoi*. Tel: 00844 828 2150, e-mail: infoEXO@exotissimo.com, go.vietnam@exotissimo.com, www.exotissimo.com
Asia Explore, Mr. Nam, 87 Nghia Thuc Str. *Ho-Chi-Minh-Stadt*. Tel. 0084-82123133/9242092, e-mail: asia-explore@vnn.vn, www.asia-explore.vn
Indochina Sails, Huong Hai Junks Co., 1 Bai Chay, *Halong City*. Tel: 0084-33845042, Hotline: 0904223626, Pier Hotline: 0904223616, e-mail: ngahuonghai@halongdiscovery.com, www.indochinasails.com

Hidden Beauties

The Hanoi – Ninh Binh – Cuc Phung Triangle

The third-largest city, the third most beautiful opera house, a first-class hotel – women at the oars, a dry bay, a national park – an unusual adventure tour.

Few roads lead to Hai Phong, but many go past. Usually the only visitors to Vietnam's largest port are simply passing through, glancing briefly at the city and rapidly resuming their journey, by car to Hanoi 100 kilometers (60 miles) away or by speedboat towards Cat Ba in Halong Bay.

However, those planning a tour of the Hanoi triangle – Ninh Binh – Cuc Phung – Hanoi – should treat themselves to a night in Hai Phong. It's likely to be a peaceful evening, because Hai Phong is widely regarded as cozy and tranquil – a lifestyle that is pretty unusual for Vietnam, but has a special charm for precisely that reason. Harbor View Hotel is the best choice, with elegant rooms and a delightful atmosphere, albeit without a view of the harbor.

The harbor itself is further away, linked to the Gulf of Tonking by 20 kilometers (12 miles) of canal. A large historic painting over the reception desk shows how things were 100 years ago. The picture inspires us to explore the old French Quarter, lined by the same trees as in the colonial era; the flame trees in red, pink, white, and violet as far as the eye can see have given Hai Phong the name "Flame Tree City." Our tour begins at Tran Phu Street, directly at the hotel. We can immediately sense how the century of colonialism left its stamp on the city. Across Boulevard de la République, now Hoang Dieu, we pass through lush gardens and arrive at the Post Office, where we can admire a lovely collection of old stamps; the post office officials are proud when we ask about them. Lined with old villas, Hoang Van Thu Street leads to the Catholic church and onward to the pretty opera house – although today, Communist Party speeches are heard there more often than operatic arias. The market, packed with enormous flower stands, is in front of the opera house, the glowing colors of the blooms vying with the dazzling fish darting to and fro in the many large aquariums at the open market stands. They form a bizarre contrast to the other commodities offered for sale – but aquarium-keeping is a widespread and very popular hobby in Vietnam. The treatment meted

1 The forgotten opera house of Hai Phong – today a meeting-place for Party members. **2** For the home aquarium – tropical fish market in Hai Phong. **3** Rowing with the feet in Dry Halong Bay. **4** Hey, what are you looking at – fish or TV?

out to the extremely expensive fish takes a little getting used to: they are packed in plastic bags and transported in stacks on a bicycle. Like a pizza delivery service, the market trader delivers the squashy bags with their flapping cargo to his customers. Of course, there's a reason for this: because the colors of the fish must harmonize with the arrangement of the aquarium, immediate exchange of the fish is included in the price if they do not suit. The market is fringed with food stalls selling delicious specialties. Foreigners are warmly welcomed and invited to make their choice from the bubbling pots to fill their rice bowls. The Vietnamese are generally highly amused: the "long-noses" turn up said noses at the best parts – chicken legs, duck heads, delicious offal.

But the cuisine of the elegant HarborView Hotel can also be highly recommended. We return past a host of small stores displaying gloriously kitschy copies of Renoir, Monet, and Van Gogh – but no tourist souvenirs. The lower corner of the triangular tour is formed by the delta of the Red River, North Vietnam's "rice bowl" district. The most scenic area is at Ninh Binh, known as "Dry Halong Bay" and dotted with conical hills, caves, and grottoes like its sister landscape at Halong Bay. They must have been created in similar ways, with the difference that here the water is distributed through long labyrinths and flows through the rice fields. It's a unique and fascinating experience to glide through the countryside in a long boat in charge of "the rowing women of Tam Coc." The high point of the trip is the tour of the Three Grottoes. The largest, Hang Hai, is 60 meters (197 feet) long and 18 meters (59 feet) wide, but may cause feelings of claustrophobia in some: it is no more than two to three meters high (7-9 feet).

Cuc Phung National Park is more spacious. Vietnam's first and only national park, it lies 45 kilometers (27 miles) westward of Ninh Binh. "Uncle Ho" himself decided in 1962 to take steps to protect the landscape, and the region is still home to an unusually diverse range of flora and fauna today. For this reason, Cuc Phung is also known as the "Vietnamese Noah's Ark." Two graves with remains from the New Stone Age prove that the forerunners of *Homo sapiens* settled here at a very early stage.

1 Decaying glory – the French Quarter in Hai Phong. **2** Delicious food, fresh salads, cheerful people – open-air food stall at the market. **3** The rowing women of Tam Coc. **4** Rice farmer in Dry Halong Bay. **5** Guide Tuan and the oldest tree in Vietnam. **6** HarborView Hotel in Hai Phong.

Touring the Hanoi – Ninh Binh – Cuc Phung Triangle

What to see

Stroll through the Old Quarter with its market and opera house. The renovated cathedral and particularly *Dinh Hang Kenh* community hall, the loveliest building in the town and covered in wood-carvings. Ninh Binh, *Tam Coc National Park*, *Dry Halong Bay*, *Cuc Phung National Park*.

Where to stay

Harbor View Hotel, Royal Garden Resort, 4 Tran Phu Street, *Hai Phong City*, Tel: 0084-31827827, e-mail: info@harbourviewvietnam.com, www.harbourviewvietnam.com
Thuy Anh Hotel, 55A Truong Han Sieu Str., *Ninh Binh Town*, Tel: 0084-30871602, mobile: 0913 518 155
e-mail: thuyanhhotel@hn.vnn.vn, www.thuyanhhotel.com

Where to eat and drink

Harbor View Hotel, Royal Garden Restaurant. Outstanding

6

cuisine for discerning guests. *Com Viet*, chic restaurant with friendly service, good food for pampered Vietnamese. The beer gardens near the theater are highly recommended for an informal evening – it's fun to lift a glass with the Vietnamese. Few tourists. Cho Ga Market has plenty of food stalls that are happy to serve special portions for European tastes.

Special recommendations

In Hai Phong it's well worth taking an extended stroll through the Old Quarter with its market and opera. The region around Ninh Binh and Tam Coc National Park is rich in natural splendor. Take a *rowing boat ride* with the "rowing women" – after recovering from the shock of the landing stage: concrete terraces and numbered positions for tourists waiting in line. At Cuc Phung landing stage, it's theoretically possible to encounter tigers. Hai Phong is generally a good starting point for excursions to Cat Ba in Halong Bay.

Information

Exotissimo Travel, Main Office, 26 Tran Nhat Duat St., *Hanoi*. Tel: 0084-48282150,
e-mail: infoEXO@exotissimo.com,
go.vietnam@exotissimo.com, www.exotissimo.com
Asia Explore Mr. Nam, 87 Nghia Thuc Str., Ho Chi Minh City. Tel: 0084-82123133/9242092, e-mail: asia-explore@vnn.vn, www.asia-explore.vn

4 5

Every Saturday in Can Cau – the Dao and Hmong peoples maintain their traditions.

Love Markets and Sugarcane

The Northern Mountain Peoples

A Visit to the North

Hanoi, Mai Chau – and the Long Trek to Sapa

"Wherever we are is the top" is a saying which fits like a glove for the mountain peoples of North Vietnam. They go about their traditional lifestyle "between heaven and earth" with assurance, wearing hand-embroidered costumes and performing traditional songs and folk dances.

There is no beginning and no end. There is only "right in the middle." Right in the middle of the most densely populated region of Vietnam. The delta of the mighty Red River is home to almost one third of the population, and every one of them seems to be on National Highway 6 between Hanoi and Mai Chau at 7 am. Yet there is never a traffic jam; everything flows smoothly and slowly – just as our thoughts do. For example, why does one village never come to an end, and the next one never seem to begin? The answer is simple: the Vietnamese always want to be in the front row, so it's a matter of life and death for them. Every household has something to offer. Noodle soup, cola, bread or special services like washing mopeds, cleaning ears or cutting hair. Because houses are built so narrow for tax reasons, there is not enough façade to display advertisements to attract customers; the enterprising entrepreneurs are forced to move as close as possible to the edge of the road in order to reach the passing trade. But anyone who has eaten soup with the deadly squeals of a tanker's double tires ringing in his ears is happy to return the spoon afterwards.
Forward-thinking food-stall owners employ special stuntmen to hurl themselves in front of vehicles from all possible positions. Milliseconds before the unavoidable crash, but only after the driver has slammed on the brakes, they smilingly hold the menu up to the window. If the asphalt artistes happen to be friends of the driver or the tour guide – what a coincidence – lunchtime is saved.
Advertising Vietnamese-style, but no matter – noodles are a feel-good food and the countryside is becoming more and more beautiful. Song Da, the Black River, has joined us along the side of the road, and the first mountains can be seen in the distance, floating in the haze over the rice fields. We still hardly notice our climb in altitude, but the clouds of diesel emitted by the overloaded trucks are growing thicker and the cyclists have moved into higher gears.

1 Wood for the hut at Son La. **2** Tea with honey in the mountains? Sure. Honey is available at the side of the road. **3** Fan dance in a stilt house – a traditional evening at Ban Lac. **4** Water buffalo in the rice fields – the poor man's tractor.

Song Da Lake, a dammed arm of the Black River 150 kilometers (90 miles) in length, starts shortly before Hoa Binh. Our pleasant tour guide for the north, whose name is Chu Tan, but who prefers to be known as Tan, not Chu, describes the sights of the region: Vietnam's largest hydropower station, a gift from the Soviets. Visitors can walk around the top of the high dam, watched over by an oversize statue of "Uncle Ho." The Hoa Binh people are believed to have inhabited the area in the New Stone Age; archeologists have found traces of prehistoric settlements.

The reason why Chu Tan prefers not to be called Chu is explained with a laugh. Foreigners tend to pronounce Chu as "shoe," which he doesn't find too funny. Tan is an excellent photographer and is happy to serve his guests as a reliable photo-op detector; he stops automatically at particularly attractive scenes in this glorious landscape – for example, just before the turnoff to Mai Chau, after an endless series of hairpin bends and switchbacks. The panoramic view over Mai Chau valley is stunning with or without a camera; we are awed at the incredible beauty of the country. The wind brings us sounds from the villages five kilometers (3 miles) away, increasing our anticipation; in the broad valley beyond Mai Chau are the villages of stilt houses where the White and Black Tai live, one of the largest of the 54 ethnic minorities living in Vietnam's mountains and uplands.

1 Stilt house with guest beds, among the White Tai at Ban Lac. **2** Everyone on the mat – extended family with international guests in their living, dining, and bedroom. **3** The harvest is over, the next one is coming – rice fields between Ban Lac and Mai Chau. **4** Preparations with child and cat – plucking herbs to improve the flavor. **5** From soup to salad, fish to meat – six-course menu in the mountain village.

Between November and March, however, the rice terraces deny us their magical emerald green. Our anticipated photos are dominated by the browns of clay soil and rice stubble, with an occasional dash of color as a Vietnamese pot-bellied pig wanders about the terraces with a bevy of piglets. Grunting, they forage in the mud with their long snouts and always find something to munch on, even if the tender shoots they crave are not available. After the harvest, the rice paddies are left to rest and attention is turned to the irrigation system or to other crops. There is plenty to do before the eternal cycle begins anew. It takes some time before the farmers have aerated the soil again, using water buffaloes and a wooden harrow straight from Biblical times. Rice farmers who are unable to afford water buffaloes, Vietnam's "poor man's tractors," use hand-drawn harrows to plough their fields. It's a tough job for the whole family, involving a permanently bent posture, and a job that buffalo owners also dread. The mighty beasts cannot be used everywhere; occasionally, the territory is too steep, too impassable or too hot. Buffaloes have their limits – these gentle animals are no

feather-light mountain goats. In addition, they are bull-headed in the truest sense and love to be made much of. The Vietnamese adore and care for their buffaloes, a task particularly enjoyed by children. The buffaloes' sensitive skin requires constant watering in hot sunshine, and as a reward for their care children are permitted to ride on their backs, lying across them and even taking a nap. A heavenly sight, and one of the most popular subjects for photographers.

Somewhere in these valleys is the cradle of the Vietnamese people. It's easy to imagine when gazing over the landscape, and there is an enchanting legend on the subject. Au Co, the princess of the mountains, encountered the dragon of the seas, Lac Long Quan. One hundred children were born of their great love, and they were to achieve immortality in their contrasting worlds of land and sea. To do this, however, they were forced to undergo a painful separation; half the children followed their father to the seas, while the other half went to the mountains with their mother. These divine children became the ancestors of the Vietnamese, who have both elements in their blood: mountains and sea.

Asphalt has long since given way to sand, and today's SUVs are actually much too wide for the little footpath between the rice fields. Just before our destination, the village of Ban Lac, comes an encounter between past and present. Which "buffalo" will back down? The driver shows enormous respect, steering into the mud and allowing the water buffalo to pass; the road to Ban Lac, a village where White and Black Tai live in traditional stilt houses on thick tree trunks, is now clear. The assembly room for the extended family is around three meters (10 feet) above the ground. The floor consists of bisected bamboo canes, with mats of plaited rice straw scarcely covering the gaps. It's a practical design ensuring excellent ventilation, and leftover food can be tipped directly into the yard through the cracks, keeping the house clean and delighting the chickens. A new house is under construction at the back of the village, brilliantly designed atop tree trunks so thick they look as if they could withstand at least one typhoon. Thick bamboo canes

serve as roof laths, thatched with reeds. The walls are of raffia and the roof can be replaced quickly if need be – a type of architecture aligned to nature that has proved its worth over generations.

Ms Nga courteously invites guests to the table, or rather to the floor, where the traditional style of eating takes place with the whole family, kith and kin, grandfather and grandmother. The large main room is the center of every aspect of daily life: eating, drinking, talking. It's the best basis from which to address even the most serious problems. The assembly around the copiously filled bowls of rice, vegetables, fish, and meat is laden with symbolism for the Vietnamese. To ensure the rice bowls can always be refilled, the family and village community must stick together – and this is demonstrated by the communal meal. Many Western visitors consider it the best memory of their stay in the village.

1 No need to be afraid of evil spirits – tour guide Chu Tan reveals the world of digital miracles. **2** On foot through the mountains to the market in Son La. **3** A balancing act between worlds – traditional hairstyle and fashionable jacket. **4** New brooms sweep clean – the ancient and traditional art of binding them. **5** Bedding down for the night in the stilt house.

Hanoi, Mai Chau – and the long trek to Sapa

What to see
On the long journey, it's worth stopping in some of the small villages of the Muong (or Dao) people along the way. Dance and song performances in the *stilt houses* at *Ban Lac*.

Where to stay
Hanoi / Mai Chau, House of Mrs. Nga, *Ban Lac*, Contact: Mrs. Nga, Tel/fax: 0084-18867378, *Mai Chau / Son La*, Cong Doan Hotel, Son La Contact: Mr. Long, Vice Director. Tel: 0084-22855314, fax: 0084-22855312.

Where to eat and drink
The restaurants in the hotels and the small food stalls en route are recommended; dinner with a family in one of the *stilt houses* at *Ban Lac* offers a unique treat, with local specialties. Breakfast – rice and soup – is unusual; baguettes can be found in Mai Chau, but tracking down coffee is difficult. Take a jar of Nescafé for emergencies.

5

Special recommendations
Dance and song with the village people. Try the bamboo dance yourself – it's fiendishly complicated to follow the simple sequence of movements and move the feet to the rhythm between the round stalks. The Vietnamese demonstrate the dance precisely, and it should work – but it never does. Tourists become hopelessly tangled in the bamboo, and fun is had by all. The delicious rice brandy is good for sweeping away inhibitions, but rather a hindrance to a polished performance. Watch as a stilt house is constructed, a stable design that can easily withstand a typhoon.

Information
Exotissimo Travel, Main Office, 26 Tran Nhat Duat St., *Hanoi*.
Tel: 0084-4 828 2150
e-mail: infoEXO@exotissimo.com,
go.vietnam@exotissimo.com,
www.exotissimo.com

None Higher

Mount Phan Si Pan, Sapa and the Smiling Hmong

The journey is shaping up to be quite an adventure: cows on the road, a moped rider asleep at the wheel, wood for the hut, blasting through to progress, a man as busy as a bee, a room with a view, and a market of love.

The hourly experiences on the long route between Mai Chau and Sapa could fill the "Specials" section of an adventure travel catalog. Cows on the road are the smallest problem – we're familiar with them from rural holidays. Blasting works are also less of a thrill when they're far away – if only the road weren't closed for hours afterwards. But things get exciting when enormous, swaying, and wobbling towers of wood appear and block the route. And it's spooky to see tiny feet and skinny legs poking out from under the mountainous stacks. A 180-degree turn solves the puzzle, revealing a face behind the tottering towers – and a pretty one at that, covered with a friendly, beaming smile. The enforced halt to pose for photographs makes the burden on the Hmong woman's back all the heavier – but her smile makes light of her heavy load.

No dramatic events are attached to the sleeping man on the moped, but it's a delightful image, and typical of the country. Vietnamese men can sleep anywhere, in any position – no chair too small, no bench too narrow. The seat of this man's Honda Dream is plenty comfortable enough for a midday siesta at the side of the road – and with that name, sweet dreams are all-inclusive. Fortunately, the blasting work on the road begins only after he has woken up again. Vietnam's progress makes its presence felt with loud explosions, ripping huge, sand-yellow scars in the lush green landscape as preparation for the construction of new roads. Behind the hill over there – is that really the future, where the new road is heading?

At any rate, this road is heading into thick fog. Instead of yellow dust, damp mist now creeps through the cracks of the jeep body, and the temperature drops. High time for hot tea with honey. It's child's play to prepare it at home – but here, in the mountains of North Vietnam? A red flag appears in the fog, waving vigorously. Another asphalt acrobat from the restaurant earlier? No, a road-

1 Vietnam's top coffee variety is Robusta – coffee plantation between Dien Bien Phu and Lai Chau. **2** The gateway to heaven – Tram Ton, the highest mountain pass in Vietnam. **3** Dream route in the mountains – taking a break on the Honda Dream. **4** New slippers at the Love Market.

side beekeeper, explains our guide Tan, and he's right. Water is quickly boiled, green tea sprinkled slowly into the pot – a dream come true – and soon we're drinking wonderfully hot, delicious tea with honey. The beekeeper, 34-year-old Do Ngoe Ban, works for the Central Beekeepers' Association. Perhaps a tough job in this isolated region, but Ban is proud of his produce, golden-yellow honey of the utmost purity.

Another 130 kilometers (78 miles) to go until Son La. Rooms have been reserved in the Trade Union Hotel. The hotel proves to be charming, and the receptionists are enchanting. I envy Tan and his assurance in flirting with them – maybe I should learn some Vietnamese?

Next morning at Son La's wonderful market, language skills are superfluous and the Esperanto of hands and feet is all that's needed – just as it is all over the world. Old Son La was almost completely destroyed in the last war in massive bombing raids by the US Army. In the previous war, from 1908, the French had established a jail for political prisoners. Fortunately, the thick walls studded with iron fetters are silent about the terrible deeds perpetrated here – a foreshadowing of Dien Bien Phu, the next stop on our journey to Sapa.

Here, then, at the edge of the modern city of Dien Bien Phu, is the hill on which the colonial rule of the French came to its final and bloody end. The museum in Dien Bien Phu provides detailed factual information on the progress of the decisive battle and its background. The memorial monuments and cemeteries for the fallen of the French and Vietnamese armies chart what remained.

The onward journey offers plenty of time for reflection; we have around 300 kilometers (180 miles) to go before the next stop in Lai Chau, around eight hours' drive through magnificent scenery on twisting roads bearing the number 12. Pleasure and reflection is easier said than done; the hairpin bends shake us into alertness, and the never-ending stream of photo opportunities entices us to stop again and again.

The terrace of La Anh Hotel in Lai Chau is occupied by a motley crew of people whose only feature in common is their desire to explore Vietnam in their own highly personal manner: an Austrian traveling on foot, two eccentric friends from the USA and England on decrepit Russian Minsk motorbikes, two German men in their sixties cycling from Hanoi. The hotel landlady runs errands on a sky-blue Italian Vespa. As international as they come – and delightfully crazy.

Our alarm call the next morning is performed by the Minsk riders, starting up their silencer-free bikes at 5.30. But that doesn't bother anyone in Vietnam – 180 kilometers (108 miles) to go before we

1 The loveliest flower in Can Cau – a 14-year-old Flower Hmong girl at the Love Market. **2** The Flower Hmong are the most colorful of all the ethnic groups. **3** Refreshment on a stick – sugarcane, a popular snack. **4** Quality control. **5** The sniggering boys make clumsy suitors.

1 Long march down from the mountains. **2** Ethnic market at Bac Ha. **3** An art student from Hanoi. **4** Checking that the cigarette lighters work. **5** Gala dinner at the mountain hotel in Sao Mai. **6** Victoria Hotel Sapa. **7** Simple accommodation with a hearty welcome at Sao Mai Hotel, Bac Ha.

see Sapa. The countryside grows more austere, the mountains become higher. Many find this section the most beautiful of the whole route. Tram Ton Pass, "the gateway to heaven," at 1,900 meters (6,230 feet) is a unique sight, and all 3,140 meters (10,300 feet) of Mount Phan Si Pan, Vietnam's highest mountain, seem close enough to touch. Bold souls with the courage to climb its summit, three to five days to spare, and a good guide at hand are richly rewarded. The view to the north extends as far as the mountains of China.

On the other side of the pass the weather changes suddenly and visibility falls to zero in the thick pea-souper fog. The only evidence that our vehicle is still following the road is the mopeds speeding past, their riders swathed in brightly colored plastic capes. How they see where they're going is a mystery to us. Finally, we see the signpost announcing Sapa, and soon after that the beautiful Victoria Hotel. A well-heated room with a view over the former health resort for the French locals is the ideal way to relax before tackling the highlight of the long journey. On the other side of the Red River, near the Chinese border, are two weekly markets that are outstanding in their attractiveness and unspoilt tradition: the "love market" in Can Cau and the ethnic market at Bac Ha. The country market of Can Cau, held on Saturdays, is a meeting point for the inhabitants of the surrounding mountain villages, who gather to haggle over prices. But the young girls who also attend have some-

2

3

4

5

thing else in mind – the boys – and if the girls find one of them to be cute, he'll need to have that made clear to him somehow. The girls don their most beautiful clothes, their most costly jewelry, and transform themselves into works of art that may be admired from a safe distance, while the boys lounge around on their mopeds and try to look cool. At first glance, the difference to mating rituals of Western teenagers is minimal, but that's what makes this affectionate observation – accompanied by a silent sigh – into a highly personal experience. We've probably all been there – and it's the same all over the world.

The ethnic market in Bac Ha takes place on Sundays, when the little village becomes the hub of the whole region. Everything that might be needed by Vietnamese mountain dwellers is offered here: ropes, nails, tools, tobacco and spices, edible creepy-crawlies – spiders – and, fortunately, fruit, too. The market is awash with a sea of bright colors, the traditional costumes of the Black Hmong with their flowers and shining silver jewelry, and the Red Dao with their red, yellow, and green headgear, varied by check prints in loud colorways. Many a fashion designer has drawn inspiration from these costumes, transporting the color sense of the North Vietnamese mountain dwellers onto the catwalks of international fashion houses.

Mount Phan Si Pan, Sapa and the smiling Hmong

What to see

Poomcoong Village, Son La market, and the former *prison at Son La*. At *Dien Bien Phu*: the *bunkers* on A1 Hill and *Dien Bien Museum*. The market at Sapa. The highlights are, without doubt, the excursions from Sapa to the markets at *Can Cau* and *Bac Ha*.

Where to stay

Son La / Dien Bien Phu, Hanoi Hotel, *Dien Bien Phu* 297A, 7/5 road. Tel: 0084-023825103, fax: 0084-23826290.
Dien Bien Phu / Lai Chau, Lan Anh Hotel 1, To 9, Song Da, *Lai Chau*.
Lai Chau / Sapa, Victoria Sapa Resort Hotel, Sapa, Contact: Mr. Ronan Bianchi (General Manager).
Tel: 0084-20871522, fax: 0084-20871539, www.victoriahotels-asia.com
Sapa / Can Cau Markt / Bac Ha Sao Mai Hotel *Bac Ha*.
Tel: 0084-20880288, fax: 0084-20780352

Where to eat and drink

After the long journey and the simple fare of the last few

days, treat yourself to the excellent restaurant at *Victoria Sapa Resort*, with wonderful candlelit Asian and French cuisine at an open fire. The service is outstanding. Down in Sapa (*Victoria Hotel* is on a hill) there is a wide choice of restaurants for all tastes and pockets. Sapa claims to have the most diverse range of cuisines in North Vietnam.

Special recommendations

Son La *market* and the former *prison* at Son La.
At *Dien Bien Phu*: the *bunkers* on A1 Hill and *Dien Bien Museum*. Take a walking tour of Sapa and stroll around the lake. But the *markets* at *Can Cau* and *Bac Ha* are definitely the highlights for visitors – and, naturally, for photography fans.

Information

Exotissimo Travel, Main Office, 26 Tran Nhat Duat St., Hanoi.
Tel: 0084-48282150,
e-mail: infoEXO@exotissimo.com,
go.vietnam@exotissimo.com,
www.exotissimo.com
Victoria Sapa Resort. Ask at Victoria Sapa Resort about hiking tours in the magnificent countryside. Excellent advice about tours for all stages of fitness, and provision of reliable guides.

Eco in Vietnam – the Logical Solution!

Hoang Lien – the Far-sighted Mountain Valley

It's not easy to combine people, nature, and tourism, but the "Eco-Lodge" is an excellent example of how it can work. Comprising 25 bungalows, the Lodge is managed and supplied by Vietnamese and provides support for the local villagers.

One of the most beautiful regions in North Vietnam, not far from Mount Phan Si Pan, Vietnam's highest mountain, contains magnificent mountain valleys with panoramic views that are unusual for Vietnam. At an altitude of over 1,500 meters (4,920 feet), the landscape that reveals itself is more reminiscent of Tyrol than of tropical forest. Here, whisper the mountain farmers, tigers still roam. The Vietnamese mountain guides smile tolerantly and lead their guests sure-footedly along the narrow mountain paths between crags, sparse vegetation, and wetly gleaming rice terraces. The Black Tai minorities who live in these regions are warm and welcoming. They traditionally live from agriculture and animal husbandry.

Two years ago, in the midst of this idyll, the Dane Jesper Kjeldsgaard realized a lifelong dream – the "Eco-Lodge." Twenty-five small cottages huddle in a semicircle on the slopes and offer visitors rustic accommodation. Everything required by the Lodge is actually produced here: power from solar cells, water from the mountain stream, vegetables and meat from the little farm above the village. The villagers' traditional agriculture has been combined with the modern power generation methods in use at the Eco-Lodge to map out new ways for tourism and tradition to merge. The Black Tai women are already joining in: twice a week they walk for hours over laborious pathways to attend English lessons in the next large village. The short, slim women in their colorful costumes are a moving sight. Chatting merrily, they make their way up hill and down dale on the road to the future – a route which must be embarked upon in partnership with these people, requiring both sides to prize social responsibility and the will to integrate in equal measure. The philosophical search for solutions is boundless. The only key is to avoid over-effusiveness; the mountain people are extremely self-assured and traditionally rooted – and they plan to remain that way.

1 Fresh from the fields – organic farmers and their fresh herbs. **2** Mountain encounter – Red Dao women. **3** Vegetable patch in front of the hut. **4** Power from the sun, water from the mountains, vegetables from the fields – the concept of the "Eco-Lodge".

The example of the English classes hits the nail on the head: the mountain people are keen to learn, and hungry to discover more about the world out there that is so eager to join up with their traditional lives.

The women there can easily imagine the benefits of foreign visitors. Young men exploit the opportunity to pass on their unique store of knowledge about their mountain home. They are outstanding hiking and climbing guides, easily on a par with their classic colleagues in Switzerland or Austria. Accompany them on a longer trip and enjoy the exhilaration. In every valley, at every altitude we encounter people with unfamiliar customs and habits who greet strangers welcomingly and, invariably, with lively curiosity. The small differences from village to village are fascinating and astonishing. The colors used for the costumes and embroidery vary from place to place, just as the forms of the silver jewelry change their shape and significance. Here, on mountain tours, "at the heart of heaven and earth," we experience intensively at first hand why Vietnam is considered the most ethnically diverse country in Southeast Asia. At the end of our journey we are better able to comprehend the recommendation made by the Vietnamese to their visitors: "Don't try to understand Vietnam – just live and breathe it and become a part of it, and it will open up for you."

We now face a two-hour drive over the twisting Deo Doc Pass to the Chinese border at Lao Cai, the bustling, noisy border town. Then the night train to Hanoi. A brief excursion along the Red River is worthwhile, to peek over the fence at neighboring China, but long lines form for a souvenir photo at the border marker with its nostalgic socialist charm of yesteryear. However, waiting is fun and offers the chance of observing people from all quarters of the globe and their behavior in front of the camera: clowning, straight-faced, serious. A crazy international comedy of manners that raises a smile and leaves a sympathetic thought behind: in some ways, people are all alike.

The thought is an effective distraction from the melancholy that threatens us at the end of this journey – and yet we bid Vietnam not farewell, but au revoir!

1 View of the mountain panorama from Hoang Lien nature reserve. **2** Wood and natural stone – the rustic architecture of the mountain huts. **3** Petroleum lamps and power from solar cells supply enough energy for the mountain restaurant. **4** Built on a slope, with a clear view over the mountains. **5** A new way forward – the "Eco-Lodge".

Hoang Lien – mountain valley with panoramic view

What to see

The whole of the *Hoang Lien valley* and its mountain villages is a single outstanding attraction for visitors. Hiking tours on sound paths over meadows and rice terraces and along mountain streams offer an encounter with nature that is rare and special.

Where to stay

Topas Eco-Lodge, 52 To Ngoc Van, *Hanoi*.
Tel: 0084-47151005-71511006,
e-mail: info@topas-adventure-vietnam.com
Victoria Train Lao Cai / Hanoi,
Contact: Mr. Ronan Bianchi (General Manager), Sapa.
Tel: 0084-20871522, fax: 0084-20871539,
www.victoriahotels-asia.com

5

Where to eat and drink

From breakfast to candlelit dinner, at the *Eco-Lodge* everything is home produce.
Vegetables come from the farm, other ingredients are supplied by local farmers. The restaurant is spacious and cozy, with many windows offering unique views over the entire valley.
Families with children can take advantage of the special menus and affectionate care.

Special recommendation

Day tours through the valley from the lodge. The majority of these tours can be taken without a guide; the panoramic view over the valley from the lodge makes it easy to identify the starting point and destination. The locals can also supply reliable information about the length of a hike, using the "pointing" method. In winter, the dry rice terraces can be used as a giant staircase – a challenge for the leg muscles.

Information

Exotissimo Travel, Main Office, 26 Tran Nhat Duat St., Hanoi.
Tel: 0084-48282150,
e-mail: infoEXO@exotissimo.com,
go.vietnam@exotissimo.com,
www.exotissimo.com

For hikes in the beautiful countryside, ask at *Victoria Sapa Resort* and in *Topas Eco-Lodge*, which offer expert advice for all levels of fitness and supply reliable mountain guides.
Victoria Train Lao Cai / Hanoi, www.victoriahotels-asia.com

Tour guide Minh Tri knows the way – to a peaceful future.

"Which Way to the War?"

Travel Tips for a Peaceful Country

Pictures, Planes, Pilots

Tracing the Footsteps of the War

Travelers encounter Vietnam's war-torn past only if they wish to – and if they so wish, they will find many opportunities to discover factual information.

From the tunnels of Cu Chi, where the only enemy threatening visitors today is claustrophobia, to the museums where tears flow as we recognize the anti-war pictures of the 1968 revolution, or the memories of Ho Chi Minh's ideology, shouting the name with raised fists: war, defeat, victory! – all these are as much a part of Vietnam's history as the imperial graves at Hue.

But war has no place in the minds of Vietnam's up-and-coming generation of today, who look to the future, eager to participate in shaping life in a country free from war. For this reason, this book has eschewed wartime imagery, choosing instead to show peaceful

1 Saigon 1967, children in a US jeep – the naive arrogance of power. **2** Air Base Da Nang 1967, China Beach, the largest US military base, with the Marble Mountains in the background. **3** Miss Saigon 1968. **4** Black Cat – ready to go. **5** Hoi An 1967 – death of a father. **6** Da Nang 2007, War Museum.

2

1

3

pictures from a four-month journey through a country of immense beauty.

I was led to this decision by my awareness of the power of images, the fascination over human tragedy and horror which they exert. War stamps itself on the memory, as I know from personal experience, but it is not necessary to have been in Vietnam to know this. Far too many people around the world carry such pictures in their minds for a lifetime.

My own personal picture from the Vietnam War dates from 1967: it is the picture of the mother and child at the father's coffin. I have never forgotten this day, or the expression on the child's face.

Finally, I overturned this power that the pictures hold – for the people of Vietnam, for their country, for those who visit them, and for myself. My hope is that in the future these scenes of tranquillity will accrue as much power as their predecessors, the images of war.

5

6

1 Can Ghio – fish rations for the Vietcong. **2** Khe San – medals for tourists. **3** Vinh Moc – a tunnel for a village. **4** Pilots' helmets at Khe San. **5** Saigon – images of war. **6** Speedboat to a Vietcong village. **7** Cu Chi – camouflaging a hideout. **8** Tien gives explanations on the tour of the demilitarized zone. **9** Thien Mui pagoda – the martyr's car.

ĐẶC ĐIỂM VỊ TRÍ CHIẾN LƯỢC
CỦA ĐƯỜNG 9 - KHE SANH
BIỂN ĐÔNG
ĐỒNG HỚI
VĨNH LINH
GIO LINH
CAM LỘ
ĐÔNG HÀ
TRIỆU PHONG
XÊ PÔN
KHE SANH
Di vật
A relic

8

9

Visiting Vietnam

Practical Travel Information

Entering the country

A tourist visa is required for all non-Vietnamese citizens and can be obtained by sending a completed application form with your original passport to your nearest Vietnamese Embassy. Your passport must be valid for at least six months from your desired date of entry to Vietnam. A tourist visa entitles you to a single stay of 14 days or one month, and can be extended at the Immigration Office in all major cities. Visas can also be obtained from:

American Embassy
7 Lang Ha Street, Hanoi
http://vietnam.usembassy.gov/visa_services.html
http://vietnam.usembassy.gov/service.html
See also: www.vietnamembassy-usa.org

British Embassy
Central Building, 4th floor, 31 Hai Ba Trung, Hanoi
http://www.britishembassy.gov.uk/vietnam
See also: http://www.vietnamembassy.org.uk/consular.html

Australian Embassy
8 Dao Tan Street, Ba Dinh District, Hanoi
http://www.vietnam.embassy.gov.au
See also: http://www.au.vnembassy.org

General information for other countries:
www.vietnam-travel.com
www.exotissimo.com

Traveling to Vietnam

Air France flies nonstop *from Paris* Charles de Gaulle to Hanoi and Ho Chi Minh City, while Eva Air offer flights to Hanoi *from London Heathrow* via Taipei.Vietnam Airlines is the only airline to fly nonstop *from Frankfurt* to Saigon and Hanoi up to 5 times weekly. British Airways currently operates three flights a day between *London Heathrow* and *Hong Kong*, enabling passengers to connect with the daily Cathay Pacific flights to Ho Chi Minh City.
United Airlines started the first American direct commercial flights to Vietnam *from San Francisco* to Ho Chi Minh City in 2007.

Other airlines, although none offering daily flights, are Air France, China Airlines, Lufthansa (Saigon only), Quatar Airways (Saigon only from March 2007), Malaysian, Aeroflot, Singapore Airlines, Korean, and Asiana. In addition, visitors can enter Vietnam from the neighboring countries of Laos, Cambodia, and the People's Republic of China.

Traveling in Vietnam

By air: the national airline, Vietnam Airlines, has an extensive network of routes and a modern fleet of aircraft – in fact, brand-new, with the exception of the ATR 72. The old Russian Antonov and Tupulev aircraft were removed from service some time ago. Shorter routes such as Saigon–Cam Ranh Bay (Nha Trang) and Phu Quoc or Rach Gia–Phu Quoc, plus Cam Ranh Bay–Danang are served by ATR 72 propeller craft, while Airbuses, Fokker 70s, and Boeing 777s are used for longer-haul flights.
Punctuality is occasionally a problem. Delays and cancellations are particularly prevalent in the typhoon season from October to December.

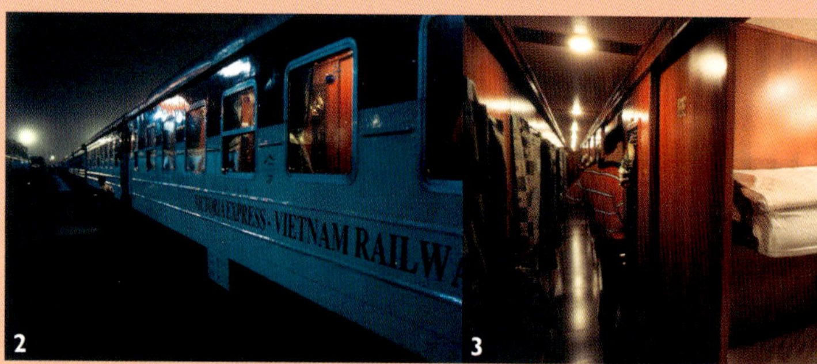

By rail: travelers planning to explore Vietnam by rail are recommended to get tickets in good time. Trains are fully booked weeks in advance, at the time of the Vietnamese New Year in particular.
Train travelers should allow plenty of time. The trains run very slowly on the often-dilapidated, single-track lines, so that you may well feel that you could easily run just as fast. And yet train travel is an ideal opportunity to come into contact with the people. There are four classes from "hard seat" to "soft sleeper." The "Reunification Train," now with air-conditioned cars, is very popular; it runs several times a day between Saigon and Hanoi, a journey time of 35–42 hours! Vietnam's most pleasant train journey is the Victoria Express from Hanoi to Lao Cai on the Chinese border.
www.victoriahotels-asia.com. Air travel is best for the stretch of almost 700 kilometers (420 miles) from Hanoi to Hue.

By bus: the local buses running between all Vietnamese cities are really only suitable for backpackers. They are so full that not even a matchstick would fit between the passengers, and they stop at every corner.
A better option is the air-conditioned coaches of smaller travel operators such as Sinh Cafe or Kim Travel. They offer the option of buying an "open bus ticket" from Saigon to Hanoi or vice versa, and adding as many stopovers to the journey as you want.
Sinh Cafe, 246–248 De Tham, Saigon. Tel: (08)8367378, www.sinhcafevn.com.
Kim Travel, 270 De Tham. Tel: (08)8369859, www.kimtravel.com.
Both offices are in Saigon's backpacker quarter Pham Ngu Lao, near Ben Thanh Market. These companies also offer tours at low prices, but including somewhat spartan accommodation.

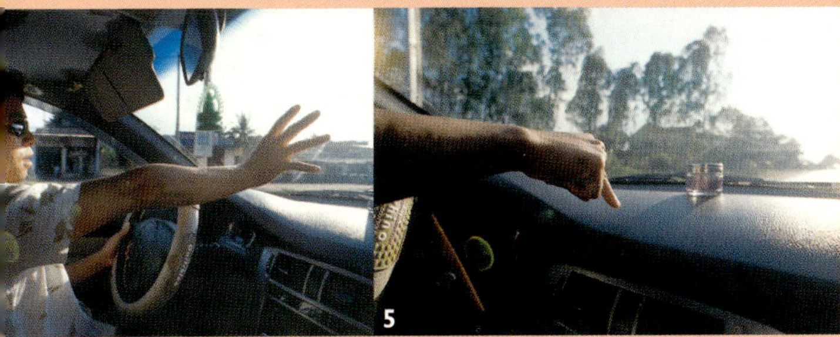

By car: traveling by car is the best and most pleasant way of getting to know Vietnam. Car hire is possible only with a driver. Foreigners are not permitted to drive, and that's just fine; while the intercity roads are much better than they were in the early 1990s, they are still crammed. And who wants to run the risk of flattening a small child or a grandmother running out in front of the car? Quite apart from the fact that the driver can also be involved in an accident. Fortunately, stricter highway laws were introduced recently. Speed checks are now common on highways, and traffic offenders receive hefty fines. Night driving should be avoided if at all possible. Moped riders must wear helmets outside cities. If you hire a car with driver, you are also responsible for paying for the driver's accommodation and any empty rides.

Mopeds: mopeds can be hired at reasonable rates all over Vietnam. However, they are not advised in major cities because of the often chaotic traffic conditions. Only experienced moped or motorbike riders should consider this method of travel. To avoid spending too much time on organizing your trip after you arrive in Vietnam, it is wise to book in advance.

If you plan to extend your vacation to take in some swimming, start your trip in North Vietnam to avoid unnecessary backtracking; North Vietnam's swimming opportunities are extremely limited.

Travel agents in Vietnam

Exotissimo Travel
Long-standing, expert travel company with branches in Saigon, Hanoi, Da Nang. 9 Dinh Tien Hoang, District 1, Ho Chi Minh City Tel: (08)8251723, fax: (08)8295800, e-mail: go.vietnam@ exotissimo.com, www.exotissimo.com
Office in the USA: Mr. Lee Marona
Exotissimo North America, Inc., 1501 N. Broadway Suite 220 Walnut Creek, CA 94596 USA. Tel: 925/937-4550,
e-mail: infoEXO@exotissimo.com

Asia Explore
Small but reliable agency specializing in every corner of Ho Chi Minh City, and tour operator throughout the country.
87 Nghia Thuc. Tel: (08)9242092, cell phone: 0903808064.
E-mail: asia-explore@vnn.vn, www.asia-explore.vn

Information in Vietnam

Hanoi

Highway4 Restaurant
Off-beat excursions into the interior, also by motorbike for pillion riders and self-drivers. 5 Hang Tre, Hoan Kiem, Hanoi
(04) 926 0693, e-mail: info@highway4.com, www.highway4.com, cell phone: 0913524658

Queen Cafe
Market leader in Hanoi for backpacker tours, 65 Hang Bac,
Tel: (04)8260860, fax: (04)8260300, www.queencafe.com.vn

General and comprehensive travel information:
www.vietnam-travel.com

Climate and travel times

Travel operators who tell you that Vietnam is pleasant all year round are not being entirely truthful. The country has a coastline of around 3,200 kilometers (1,920 miles). Travelers planning to visit the whole country in a single vacation simply cannot expect to have good weather all the time. Your motto should be "Less is often more."
In North Vietnam, the best time to travel is September to November. Temperatures are generally pleasantly warm, around 25 °C (77 °F), and it is dry. In the mountainous north, temperatures drop dramatically in December. While the spring, March-April, is warmer, extended heavy rain and drizzle are frequent.

Central Vietnam: the best time to travel is from January to mid-September. In October to December, occasional typhoons and heavy, day-long rainfall may occur. Visitors may get wet feet in cities such as Hue or Hoi An, or at the bathing resorts of Nha Trang and Mui further south.

South Vietnam: best time to travel is January to April.

1 Lao Cai, the Chinese border. **2** Night train to Hanoi – the Victoria Train. **3** Luxury berth in the swaying train. **4** Secret signs to oncoming traffic: "All right, no police here." **5** Hand signal for "Watch out, police about." **6** Rain in the Mekong Delta. **7** "Phoning home" – not only for ET – Internet in Vietnam, Dalat Palace Hotel.

Tet, the New Year celebration, is the most important holiday for the Vietnamese. It takes place some time between mid-January and mid-February, determined by the lunar calendar. While *Tet* is certainly a unique experience for visitors, the Vietnamese are far too busy celebrating themselves to have time to look after the "long-noses." Many Vietnamese living abroad return to visit their families at *Tet*. During this period many restaurants are closed, flights and hotels are fully booked, and prices of accommodation, restaurants, and transport double. Many hotels serve an obligatory and expensive set holiday meal.

Safety

Vietnam is one of the safest countries in the world for travelers. Violence against foreign visitors is extremely rare, since the government imposes severe punishment in such cases, but visitors should beware of pickpockets in the major cities of Saigon and Hanoi. It is unwise to travel by cyclo (bicycle taxi) late at night. Taxis are cheap. Please ensure that the taxi driver switches on the meter. It is wise to deposit all valuables such as passports, air tickets, credit cards, and money in the room safe of your hotel, if possible, or at the reception desk, and only take enough money for your daily needs.

Emergency telephone numbers

Police 113, fire brigade 114, ambulance 115

Telephoning

The country code for Vietnam is 0084, followed by the area code without the zero and then the subscriber number. Vietnam also has low-cost prefix dialing – save money by dialing 17100 before the telephone number you want. You can also do this from your hotel room. Cell phones may be used in larger cities but costs are high; it is more sensible to buy a prepaid card in a phone store (e.g. Vinaphone). Telephoning is then far cheaper with a Vietnamese number. The Internet is particularly popular with young Vietnamese, and Internet cafés offering surfing at extremely low rates can be found on every street corner.

Traffic

Traffic in Vietnam is often chaotic, particularly in Saigon and Hanoi. The streets are teeming with mopeds. To cross the street, move slowly and continuously and never stop abruptly. Conditions are improving slowly; most moped riders will even stop at red traffic lights.

Money

The euro is becoming more and more widespread in Vietnam, with exchange rates slightly more favorable for 50-euro and 100-euro notes than for smaller notes. All international airports have banks with exchange facilities.
Money can also be changed at hotel reception desks, at rates only slightly lower than those of the banks. Jewelry stores are also happy to change money. There is no black market for currency.
1 US dollar is currently (as of November 2007) worth around 16,300 Vietnamese dong, and 1 GB pound is worth 33,470 dong. 1 euro is currently worth around 21,000 dong (easier to remember as 1 euro = 20,000 VND). In major cities, money can be withdrawn from automatic teller machines (ATMs) by credit card or EC card with PIN (up to 2 million dong per transaction, just under 100 euros, 62 GB pounds or 126 US dollars. Most hotels, stores, galleries, and higher-class restaurants accept the main credit cards.

Health

Tap water should not be drunk. Mineral water can be bought everywhere – check that the seal on the bottles is unbroken. Higher-class hotels supply mineral water free of charge. At the beach, please do not eat seafood sold by beach sellers. It may look appetizing, but occasionally unsold goods from the previous evening reappear for sale the next day. Seafood is always fresh and safe to enjoy in restaurants. Vaccination against hepatitis A and B, tetanus, rabies, and polio is recommended. Malaria: travelers should consult doctors or tropical institutes to decide whether to take preventive or standby medicine. Risk of malaria can be reduced by taking a daily dose of vitamin B1, which mosquitoes dislike, and by using mosquito repellent at twilight and sunrise. Avian influenza: please stay away from live poultry.

Filming, photographs, electricity

We recommend taking an adequate supply of films from home, since films are easy to find in Vietnam, but have often been stored in over-warm conditions. Vietnamese are generally happy to be photographed, but please ask permission beforehand or confirm permission by means of gestures. Do not photograph the Red Dzao in the northern mountains – they believe that they will lose their soul when photographed. The mountain peoples in North Vietnam occasionally ask for something in return for a photograph; buy a trifle from them.
Vietnam has 110/220 volts AC. Most electric power sockets correspond to the European norm, but bring a travel adapter for the area north of Hanoi.

Clothing

We recommend light, cellular cotton clothing. Visitors to North Vietnam should also pack warm clothing, good shoes, and waterproof rainwear. Most hotels offer a fast, cheap cleaning service.

Excess baggage

It's very tempting to bring home souvenirs – and very shocking at the airport when the cost of the excess baggage is counted up. Air France is extremely strict, demanding a hefty payment of 23 euros (16 GBT, 30 US $) per kilogram for every gram over the baggage allowance. Other airlines are a little more flexible: Lufthansa is very much more accommodating, and Thai is open to negotiation – but do not rely on this. However, sometimes a courteous telephone call a few days before departure can solve the problem. Baggage allowance for economy class: 20 kilos; business class: 40 kilos.

The Vietnamese People

The Vietnamese are generally extremely open, friendly people. There are few countries where contact with the people is easier. The Vietnamese are extremely hospitable, to the point of inquisitiveness; do not be surprised if they ask highly personal questions. Vietnamese love to laugh. The country is suffused with the sense of a new beginning; people rarely think of the past, concentrating instead on the present and future. They prefer not to be questioned about the war.
Tourists are occasionally fleeced when buying souvenirs on the street. If an argument arises (e.g. when haggling over a price), do not raise your voice, but argue in a calm and business-like tone. Overreacting is seen as loss of face, and open impatience will not help. Travelers planning to take a cyclo should always agree on a price in advance to avoid unpleasant surprises. An hourly rate of 20,000 dong serves as a rule of thumb, although locals pay considerably less. If you have business cards, present them with both hands.
The Vietnamese set store by neat clothing, particularly in temples and pagodas. Main things to remember: never allow the soles of your feet to face anyone, and never wave someone over to you in European style.

1 "Madame et Monsieur, dinner is served," a tour of Da Lat, Palace Hotel. **2** "Pigging out" – the Tet Festival begins – 2007 was the Vietnamese Year of the Pig.

Main public holidays

3 February: founding of Vietnamese Communist Party
30 April: Reunification Day or Liberation Day, commemorating the liberation of Saigon from the US Army
19 May: Birthday of Ho Chi Minh
2 September: Declaration of independence from French colonial rule.
Buddhist holidays are based on the lunar calendar. The main festivals are Buddha's birthday or *wesak* in the spring and the Feast of Wandering Souls in the summer.

Tet Festival

The *Tet* Festival is the most important event in Vietnam. A family festival comparable to our Christmas, it lasts for seven days, five of which are given over to intensive celebration. During this time, banks, official institutions, many stores and restaurants are closed. *Tet* is the beginning of the New Year, according to the Chinese lunar calendar, and falls between mid-January and mid-February. It is also a festival of cleansing, and houses and temples are scrubbed days beforehand. And it is a festival of flowers. In the days leading up to *Tet*, whole streets are decorated with apricot and mandarin trees and branches of peach blossom. The first days of the festival are dedicated to visiting family, neighbors, and friends, and accompanying them to temples and pagodas. On the last evening of the old year, families gather at their ancestors' shrines to thank and commemorate them. Almost all Vietnamese worship their ancestors, decorating the altars with fresh fruit, a glass of rice wine, and rice cakes and lighting incense sticks. They present each other with brand-new banknotes in red envelopes – red being the color of good fortune. Everything that happens in the first few hours of the New Year is interpreted as a good or bad omen for the year ahead. Many Vietnamese are delighted to welcome a foreign visitor as the first to cross their threshold in the New Year, believing that they bring good luck and wealth.

Top tips in Vietnam

What you absolutely must see:

Halong Bay
Enjoy a cruise through the Bay of the Descending Dragon on a traditional wooden junk.

Tam Coc National Park
Fascinating karst landscape to explore by rowing boat, generally paddled by women using their feet.

Mountainous North
A visit to the climatic spa of Sapa and the market of the mountain people in Bac Ha are unique experiences. Encounters with ethnic minorities.

Hoi An
A stroll through the Old Quarter of Hoi An, where Asian and European cultures meet.

Adventure in the Mekong Delta
Boat rides along narrow rivers and floating markets in Vietnam's rice bowl region. Visit the floating houses where pangasius fish are farmed.

Phu Quoc tropical island
Picturesque beaches, pepper plantations, and idyllic fishing villages are the main features of this island paradise.

INDEX

Researching Saigon – author Jochen Voigt goes about his business with city experts Nam and Vy.

Persons

Places

Hotels

Credits

Author and photographer:
In his twenties, author Jochen Voigt was a war photographer in Vietnam in 1967/68. Visiting the country forty years later, he suddenly realized that throughout his career as a photographer, cameraman, and TV scriptwriter, no country had absorbed him more intensively and enduringly than Vietnam. Today he knows that it is the Vietnamese people who have always fascinated him. People with unique courtesy and openness, and with an infectious witty charm that conveys their zest for life. It is to these people and their country that Jochen Voigt dedicates this book.

Jacket photos:
Front: Nha Trang, Ana Mandara Resort (large picture); at the love market in Can Cau, courtyard of Thien Hau pagoda, Saigon street scene (top, from left to right).
Front flap: The author with his "Vietnam Leica"
Back: At Chau Doc

Picture credits:
All photographs by Jochen Voigt with the exception of:
Front jacket, large picture: Selbach/laif, Cologna; page 124, Mr. Cu, page 125 Doug Young

Acknowledgements:
My thanks to everyone who believed in this book and in my work during the long and not always easy months in Vietnam. Special thanks go to Patanida Jantsakool from Exotissimo in Saigon, who helped me to share the main burden. Our cooperation was based on trust, not on signed contracts, and was an enormous reserve of strength for my work. My thanks to Lufthansa in Hamburg: not a cent to pay for my excess baggage. "Make sure the book turns out well!" Thanks, I certainly will. – Real old-fashioned service.

Lufthansa

My thanks to Thai Airways, Frankfurt, for dealing with my excess baggage on the flight to Vietnam, and to Thai's Bangkok office for the surprise farewell gift.

We are always grateful for suggestions and advice. Please send your comments to:
C.J. Bucher Publishing,
Product Management
Postfach 80 02 40
81602 Munich Germany
e-mail:
editorial@bucher-publishing.com
www.bucher-publishing.com

Translation: Alison Moffat-McLynn, Munich, Germany
Proofreading: Danko Szabo, Munich, Germany
Design: Werner Poll, Munich, Germany, revised by Thomas Übelacker, Munich, Germany
Cartography: Astrid Fischer-Leitl, Munich, Germany
Product management for the German edition: Joachim Hellmuth
Product management for the English edition: Dr. Birgit Kneip
Production: Bettina Schippel
Repro: Repro Ludwig, Zell am See, Austria
Printed in Slovenia by MKT Print

ISBN 978-3-7658-1629-1